manifesto

The Empire and Ukraine *revisited*
Andrew Murray

Published in 2023 by Manifesto Press

© Andrew Murray

All rights reserved. Apart from fair dealing, e.g. for the purpose of private study or research, no part of this publication may be reproduced or transmitted, in any form or by any means, electronic, photocopying, recording or otherwise, without the prior permission of the copyright owner.

All rights reserved

ISBN 978-1-907464-54-6

Typset in Bodoni and Gill

Contents
2 Introduction to 2023 Edition *Empire and Ukraine revisited*

4 *Empire and Ukraine 2022*

24 *The Empire and Ukraine*
31 Part One   21st Century Imperialism
66 Part Two   The Ukraine in five questions
101 Part Three   The Left and Ukraine
116 Conclusion

118 Bibliography

Introduction to 2023 Edition

ONE YEAR into the Russo-Ukraine-NATO war or, if you prefer, nine years into the conflict sparked by the Maidan coup in Kyiv, military developments still look unlikely to bring matters to a speedy conclusion.

On the one hand, battle tanks by the dozen are on their way to Ukraine from NATO countries, including Britain. Fighter jets may follow, as the US and Britain double down on the conflict amidst billowing clouds of Churchillian rhetoric.

On the other hand, a Russian offensive is expected. Hundreds of thousands of conscripts have now had rifles shoved in their hands and are apparently ready to extend the area of Ukraine already seized by Putin.

Neither development is likely to be decisive. Both sides appear sufficiently armed and equipped to be able to avoid losing. Likewise, Moscow and Kyiv (with Washington and London at its elbow) both believe that they have more to gain by continued fighting than by attempting to negotiate a settlement.

How could the war then end? Perhaps Putin will at some point declare that he has achieved his shape-shifting objectives, or at least has secured sufficient additional territory, to declare an end to offensive operations. That would not satisfy Ukraine of course, but Russia would then be enable to entrench in powerful defensive positions from which Ukraine could not expect to dislodge them, setting the stage for some sort of winding down of the conflict eventually.

The same point could be reached if Ukraine's own offensives in 2023 are unable to reproduce the successes of 2022 around Kharkov and Kherson and therefore ceases, in the eyes of its western sponsors, to any longer look like a credible victor.

It is also possible that the lavishly-rearmed Ukrainian forces could continue to advance slowly and do such attritional damage to Putin's forces that Moscow eventually, with or without Putin still in place, decides to cut its losses.

None of these seem immediately likely. And none would, in any case, provide a basis for an enduring peace. Any settlement attained through exhaustion alone would merely constitute a pause before a resumption of conflict.

That is for compelling political reasons. The nationalist forces in Ukraine, who are also largely neo-liberal forces and enjoy the sponsorship of Washington and London, have been reinforced by the war as one might have expected and have in any case taken coercive measures against all dissent and opposition. They will not be dislodged soon.

Likewise, any move against the Putin regime is far more likely to come from the nationalist right in Russia rather than a liberal or anti-war opposition which wants for public support and is, again, under the cosh of prophylactic repression.

The other route to peace – mass independent working-class action in both Ukraine and Russia - looks even less plausible alas. Most of the left and trade unions in both countries are firmly tied to their "own" ruling classes, marginal forces aside.

That gives the anti-war movement particular problems but particular responsibilities too. With nothing but deadlock looming on the battlefield – a prediction which could of course be falsified but only with a considerable shock – the peace talks which are the obvious alternative will require concerted international pressure above all.

Most of the world wants such a solution from China to Brazil, India to South Africa, Saudi

Arabia to Iran even – none want to support NATO's war to the knife against Russia, and all cautiously seek to circumvent the Washington-ordered sanctions which are disrupting the world economy.

But the British labour movement does not. Keir Starmer, echoed by some useful idiots on the left, stands to the right of the British government in some respects on this issue, has not merely endorsed NATO without reservation but prohibited any of his MPs from dissenting from this bovine bellicosity.

This is the front we in Britain need to be fighting on – developing a peace axis that can contribute to ending the war and also challenge the ideology of authoritarian imperialism that animates Starmer and company.

Most of this book was written in 2014-15 in the aftermath of the Maidan coup, the Russian annexation of Crimea and the uprising in the Donbas. A few polemical appendices, now dated, have been removed, and replaced by the 2022 update written after the Russian invasion.

The intellect supposes that this may not be the last revision required by events, yet the will urgess that no further updates will be needed, unless it is to recognise the development of a durable peace.

Andrew Murray
February 2023

Introduction

Stop the War Coalition has warned for many years that the wars of the early twenty-first century in Iraq, Afghanistan and Libya, were likely to be precursors to still more threatening great power clashes.

So much was observable from precedence, and from the contours of world politics as they emerged in the post-Cold War world.

With the war in Ukraine that point of transition has been reached. One great power, Russia, has invaded its neighbour on the grounds that it was becoming the military instrument of a rival power bloc. That bloc, NATO led by the USA, has accordingly mobilised against Russia. Two wars in one are therefore taking place – a war waged by Russia against Ukraine, and a "proxy war" pitching NATO against its rival. As this is written, the second is subsuming the first.

The present author first predicted a great power clash over Ukraine in a book published in 1997.[1] Its likelihood has been patent since 2014, when Ukrainian politics were convulsed by a nationalist coup against an elected government and Russia first annexed territory from its neighbour. A further book analysed those events.[2] Now the projected conflict has come to pass its issue is uncertain. One hundred days in neither side appears able to definitively prevail on the battlefield, nor to concede that it cannot. Those in Washington and London who favour a prolonged war to debilitate Russia appear to be ascendant. The urgent need is for a ceasefire and negotiations, something the British government explicitly aims to obstruct, preferring war to bleed a rival. More and more powerful weapons are being shipped into Ukraine to that end.

A great power conflict is different from the wars against which the anti-war movement has hitherto mobilised this century. Iraq, Afghanistan and Libya (and indeed the earlier war against Yugoslavia) bore a neo-colonial stamp. They pitched a consortium of established imperialist powers against much weaker countries. Britain has invariably been among the military aggressors. The focus for Stop the War was plain.

Yet those conflicts, dreadful as they were and with ramifications which resonated far and wide, and to this day, never threatened to become a global conflict. There was no talk of nuclear weapons (except in relation to the ones Iraq never had). Their economic consequences were generally more limited to the victim country.

The Ukraine war, by contrast, remains fraught with the possibility of escalation. Already it has led to huge arms transfers, pledges of massive increases in defence spending, the eastward deployment of western armies, food shortages in parts of the world and an increase in energy prices for already hard-pressed working people. There has been demonstrative talk about nuclear weapons.

It also divides the world along new lines. Few support Russia's original invasion but many states, including the largest, maintain a studied neutrality between the warring powers. The "international community" invoked by Boris Johnson and Joe Biden is not much more than a NATO-plus. The drift into new competing blocs, still embryonic outside NATO, will advance. The alliance between Russia and China is the most potent sign of this.

This is the new, and fast-changing, "order" which will succeed the decades of US unipolar power. That power is passing (see Afghanistan) yet still potent (see the response to the Ukraine invasion). What succeeds it is moot. But everything in history tells us that such a period of transition is a moment of greatest danger, when the menace of great-power wars casts the longest shadow.

The anti-war movement needs to reorient in this environment. It does so under more hostile political fire than previously, most of it coming from the epigones of social democracy, imperialism's stalwart bulwark. The British government has been just about the most bellicose on the planet in the present crisis, but not so bellicose that Keir Starmer's "official opposition" cannot see it and raise.

This pamphlet seeks to expand on these points, and develop the arguments set out in *Empire and Ukraine* in the light of the renewed conflict.

Putin's war

The reasons for, and objective of, the Russian invasion of Ukraine, starting from February 2022, have had a somewhat shape-shifting character. To a point, they can be extracted from statements made by President Putin, and to some extent they must be inferred from the course of military operations.

The initial stated aim was to "demilitarise and denazify" Ukraine. The former was not defined – it could not seriously be taken to mean that Ukraine should have no military capacity at all, so it is best understood as removing any possibility of Ukraine posing a military threat to Russia, or allowing itself to be used by others with that in mind. These concerns had a certain amount of substance.

"Denazify" has more of a propaganda flavour – there are indeed Nazis in Ukraine, some of them embedded within the state apparatus, but they do not dominate its political life, a role actually reserved for the USA. A larger body of opinion celebrates Ukrainian nationalists who collaborated with Nazis during World War Two but does not propose to install a Hitler-type regime today. How the "special military operation", to use the Putinesque term, was going to address this was not clear at the outset and is no clearer today. The destruction of the notorious Azov battalion in and around Mariupol may count as a step in that direction, but such bodies have plenty of scope and incentive to reform in the rest of Ukraine, and will doubtless do so.

It is fair to conclude that these two objectives were really synonyms for regime change. Indeed, Putin himself urged the Ukrainian military to overthrow the Zelensky government in the first days of the conflict, on the grounds that the former would be easier to cut a deal with. The large-scale deployment of Russian troops around Kyiv likewise spoke of a plan to decapitate the Ukrainian state, either to introduce a new government based around Russian-sympathetic Ukrainian politicians, or possibly to terminate Ukrainian statehood in toto in favour of new arrangements. Some Russian statements did indeed call into question Ukraine's sovereignty altogether, just as Putin has cast doubt on the existence of a distinct Ukrainian people.

Since Russia's political reach exceeded its military grasp the Kyiv offensive speedily stalled and was abandoned, the Russian army retreating amid revelations of atrocities against civilians which, while quite possibly exaggerated, are almost certainly real. Such atrocities are the inevitable corollary of occupying territory where the population does not want you, and there is no reason to expect the Russian army to be an exception to this logic of brutalisation.

Yet at the same time as bruiting the possibility of regime change, the Putin government also opened negotiations with the Ukrainian government, suggesting a twin-track strategy. These focussed on two issues, Ukrainian neutrality, and its territorial integrity in relation to Russian-speaking areas. We shall turn to these shortly. With the reversal around Kyiv it became clear that the conflict would eventually have to terminate with an agreement between the Ukrainian and Russian governments, absent internal developments in Russia leading to a collapse of that regime instead, a perspective which does not seem likely enough to form the basis for a strategy.

There has been a lot of speculation as to why Putin ordered the invasion when he did. He may have run out of patience with the failure of the Kyiv government to honour the Minsk agreements on resolving the Donbas crisis, signed in 2015. There is an argument that he was exasperated by Zelensky's persecution of pro-Russian politicians and media, which was foreclosing Russia's political options and making military action the only remaining means to secure his objectives. And he had to do something with his army once he had parked it on Ukraine's borders – withdrawal with his demands unmet would have been an unthinkable humiliation.

Less plausible arguments include the idea that the Ukrainian army was about to launch an offensive against the Donbas – it seems highly improbable that it would embark on such an adventure with 150,000 Russian troops on its doorstep, a force which, had it been deployed exclusively in the Donetsk and Luhansk "independent republics" rather than divided between half a dozen different fronts would in any case have been more than sufficient to repulse intruders. There was it is true an escalating number of ceasefire violations along the Donbas front and some larger impending US-initiated provocation cannot be discounted, but in fact such a thing had not yet occurred.

Neither does it seem likely that Putin felt his own position threatened by the development of a democratic Ukraine, since such a development is awaited rather than accomplished, and the Russian state appears presently adequate to defending its positions against its own people as required.

Putin's own elaboration on his plans has traded heavily on the idea that Ukrainians and Russians are one people, that the former have no distinct history and hence no right to self-determination, indeed that self-determination, at least as it applies within the former Tsarist Empire, was a Bolshevik perversion of no political value. His address on the subject directly before the invasion began was replete with attacks on Lenin and Bolshevism, something that the cod-Leninists who endorse his war would have done well to pay more attention to. His arguments bear a close resemblance to those of 19th century imperialism, and certainly offer no basis for the conduct of contemporary international politics.

Nevertheless, the Mark Two rationalisation for the war, once storming Kyiv had been abandoned, was the protection of the Russian or Russian-speaking people of the Donbas, swaddled in historical mysticism in Putin's telling. In this second phase, military operations more-or-less correlated with political objectives (not to mention the Russian army's actual capacities) and were directed towards establishing Russian control over the entirety of the Donbas, only one-third of which had hitherto lain within the territory of the "independent republics", as well as wider stretches of territory in the south of the country. These latter conquests, in regions within which the Russian-sympathetic population is a much smaller proportion of the whole than in Donbas, both establish a land bridge to the Russian-annexed (in 2014) Crimea, and effectively cut Ukraine off from the sea. How much of this Putin intends to retain control of and how much is held as negotiating leverage remains to be seen.

Three months in, it seems that miscalculations abound. An over-estimation of Russian military capabilities, and a symmetrical under-estimation of the strengthening of the Ukrainian state since 2014, and its capacity and will to resist. Sympathy for Russia amongst the peoples of Ukraine, at least outside relatively small areas, has also been misjudged. As Boris Kagarlitsky has wisely noted, there are many in eastern Ukraine who might have been content to be governed from Moscow, but very many fewer who wish to be bombed by it. Political expectations have gone awry. Whatever the final resolution on the battlefield, the outcomes from the war seem likely to be deeply damaging to Russia itself. The integration of Finland and Sweden into NATO is only the down-payment on this disaster. Ukraine itself may have expedited entry into the European Union, which has its own defence dimension. The old saw that it is "worse than a crime, it is a blunder", applies.

But it is also a crime. No United Nations sanction for the action was as much as sought. Like Bush and Blair in 2003, Putin regarded it as superfluous. Neither aggression against Russia itself, nor genocide of Russian-speakers was imminent, or perhaps even contemplated. Ironically, many Russian-speakers in Mariupol and elsewhere who have survived the last eight years under Maidan Ukraine will have succumbed to Russia's siege. The tens of thousands of deaths, the more than ten million refugees driven from their homes and the vast destruction in Ukraine wrought by Russia's attack have no justification. Frustration with a neighbour's recalcitrance and distaste for its putative alliances do not meet the threshold for a just war. Ukrainians have a right to resist the obliteration of their state and the negation of their identity. An anti-war movement that does not say these things would be no anti-war movement at all.

Of course, the western response is high on hypocrisy. That argument can cut both ways, however. The USA would not tolerate a hostile Mexico, or a Mexico forming a military pact with China, it is said. Doubtless true. But if the US then invaded its southern neighbour would the anti-war movement say "fair enough"? Of course not. It would champion Mexico's sovereignty.

Unjustified, however, does not mean unprovoked. Here is the west's greater responsibility for the war.

NATO's expanding empire

NATO is, in British politics at least, the great unmentionable of the war. Merely alluding to its background role in shaping the current calamity is to invite social media invective and, in the event you are a Labour MP, the threatened loss of your job.

Nevertheless, Hamlet must have its Prince. NATO is central to the story, Keir Starmer's anathemas notwithstanding. Founded as a pillar of post-war capitalist order with a dual function of applying military pressure on the Soviet Union and the socialist community of the day, while also integrating the main European capitalist powers into a bloc under US hegemony it has undergone a three-fold transformation since its original mission as rendered otiose by the collapse of the USSR in 1991.

First, it has expanded – famously so. Although US leaders promised the enfeebled leaders of the Soviet Union that the alliance would expand "not one inch" eastwards once the symmetrical Warsaw Pact was disbanded and Soviet troops withdrawn to their homeland, it is likely that they never intended to be bound by the pledge. Since then, taking the view that Russia could noisily object but not do anything about it, it has relentlessly incorporated one country after another, including every Warsaw pact member state in Eastern Europe and the three former Soviet republics by the Baltic.

Here it may be objected that the accession of these states was the wish of democratically-elected governments, concerned about the possibility of Russian revanchism and wanting to make nice with all-powerful Washington anyway. However, there is no automatic right to join any military alliance or bloc. The end of the Cold War was the opportunity to dissolve them and put in their place a new pan-European security architecture protecting all but dominated by none. That was not the US plan, which preferred to see its own hegemony expanded as far as possible and for as long as possible. The decision to push NATO east was undoubtedly a provocation, and consistent with publicly-advertised US plans to prevent any restoration of Russia as a world power. Wiser heads, including the ideologist of the original Cold War US diplomat George Kennan, warned against this provocative hubris, but to no avail.

Secondly, NATO turned overtly aggressive. NATO per se had not engaged in any direct military action during the Cold War. The endless wars of the USA (and Britain) were fought under other auspices. But freed from the logic of bipolar confrontation, NATO leapt into action. The bombing of Yugoslavia in 1999 was launched under its umbrella, despite the fact that no NATO member was remotely threatened by events in Serbia. Likewise, the disastrous and humiliating twenty-year occupation of Afghanistan was a NATO project. And when the Libyan state was destroyed in 2011 in another enduring calamity, it was NATO which supervised the destroying.

The war in Iraq was not a NATO enterprise, given the staunch opposition of France and Germany to the aggression, but it is now almost universally acknowledged as an illegal war of choice by the leading NATO powers, the USA and Britain. Anyone who now tries to argue that NATO is exclusively a "defensive alliance" cannot really keep a straight face while doing so.

Third, the concept of "north Atlantic" has been stretched beyond breaking point, as the above litany of interventions indicates. NATO has gone global, deploying its overwhelming military power wherever it chooses, irrespective of geography. So taking all this together, Russian concerns at its triple-decked expansion cannot be dismissed as irrational.

Putin started explicitly flagging Russia's primordial anxieties about NATO's eastward march in 2007, just a few years after he had floated the possibility of joining it, to then-President Clinton's embarrassment. The response by hubristic Washington was to promote its still-further expansion the next year, this time to two further ex-Soviet republics, Georgia and Ukraine. The drive to bring Ukraine, by far the largest and most industrially-developed piece of the old USSR other than Russia itself, into the orbit of the US, was key to the dual project of preventing any reassertion of Russian power while entrenching US domination of Europe.

Initially, little was done to give effect to this fresh expansion at a formal level – Ukraine hardly progressed towards actual NATO membership. However, the policy was repeatedly reaffirmed by Kiev and Washington alike, and was buttressed by substantial bilateral military accords between the two governments, most recently in autumn 2021 which clearly advanced US power closer to Russia's borders. A long fuse had been lit. Ukraine is the powder keg at the other end.

Divided Ukraine

Ukraine arrived rather late at the nationalism party. Its most ardent proponents cannot identify much in the way of a Ukrainian national consciousness before the end of the nineteenth century, and even than it was not more than embryonic. That there was a Ukrainian people, with their own language and cultural referents, was undoubted. But its mainly peasant population, divided between the Tsarist Empire and the Austro-Hungarian, had a very limited conception of itself as constituting a nation. As ever, a thin layer of nationalist intellectuals played a key part in catalysing its development. Ukrainian nationalism was "a folly of a few dozen petit bourgeois intellectuals, without the slightest roots in the economic, political or psychological relationships of the country", according to Rosa Luxemburg.[3]

The obstructions in the way of the formation of a Ukrainian nation-state were formidable. Not only were Ukrainian lands divided between the two empires, the part in Austria-Hungary was itself subdivided between areas of Austrian and Hungarian control in that dysfunctional Heath Robinson-esque political structure. Moreover, across these territories Ukrainians mingled with other peoples – Russians, Poles and Jews most of all. As a rule, the Ukrainians populated the countryside, while Russians Jews and Poles preponderated in the cities.

The First World War started to transform the picture, with the disintegration of rotten imperial edifices across the continent which it caused. The February 1917 revolution unleashed centripetal movements across the Tsarist Empire. A first Ukrainian state was established as a German puppet regime after the Treaty of Brest-Litovsk was signed with the Bolsheviks. A far more significant polity was the Ukrainian Peoples Republic (UPR), which sought to unite western and eastern Ukraine in a common state which flickered off and on amidst the vicissitudes of a multi-sided war with armies (nationalists, Reds, Whites, Polish, anarchists) sweeping back and forth across its territory, contesting sovereignty with Soviet Ukraine above all. It is interesting to note that the lands claimed by this republic included most of contemporary Ukraine and significant elements of what is now Russia or Belarus – but not Crimea, the Donbas, or Galicia in the west. The republic was the site of a horrific wave of pogroms in these years, the liberal intentions of the UPR leadership notwithstanding, in many ways the first act of the Holocaust.

When all this dust had settled, Ukrainian-peopled lands were more divided than ever. The bulk constituted a Soviet republic, ultimately governed by Moscow as the capital of the socialist federation. Significant territory ended up in the new and bloated Polish state, which incorporated eastern Galicia (ex-Austria-Hungary) and Volhynia (ex-Russian Empire). Smaller chunks in the west and south were taken by Rumania (North Bukovina and Southern Bessarabia) and Czechoslovakia (Transcarpathia).

Soviet Ukraine, bolstered by the adhesion of the more proletarian but mainly Russian Donbas mining and steel-producing region, was initially a focus for the development of Ukrainian national culture, a process somewhat reversed in the 1930s, which also saw the republic suffer grievously from a famine associated with the collectivisation of agriculture and the USSR's accelerated industrial development.[4]

World War Two saw the consolidation of the Ukrainian lands into a common political structure for the first time. The Polish-occupied lands were annexed in 1939, a move initially welcomed by the Ukrainian and Jewish populations there. The Romanian-governed territories followed in 1940. These were all re-included in the USSR in 1944 and 1945. In 1945, Transcarpathian Ukraine was added to the Soviet republic, having in the meantime been detached from Czechoslovakia by fascist Hungary, and then reattached to the former.

The war also had the subordinate character of a civil war in Ukraine (a second one in twenty-five years in effect), a fact which resonates in Ukrainian politics to this day. Germans swept east through the republic in 1941, and the Red Army swept through west again in 1943-44. Ukrainian nationalism thought it saw its moment and sought to establish a notional independence under the Nazis, who were not terribly interested in this daydream of Slavic untermenschen. So the Organisation of Ukrainian Nationalists, led by Stepan Bandera, and its associated military formations fought prolonged combat against the Red Army, Poles and, much more occasionally, Germans in pursuit of the chimera of an ethnically-homogenous Ukrainian state. To that end, Ukrainian nationalists massacred around 100,000 Polish civilians. They also assisted enthusiastically in the Holocaust of Jews in Ukraine. Indeed, no peoples subjected to the Nazi Empire rendered greater service to Hitler in this respect. However, it should never be forgotten that the largest part of the Ukrainian people resisted the Nazis, and the greatest number of Ukrainians bearing arms did so in the Red Army, reluctant though post-Maidan Ukrainian leaders are to acknowledge this.

These divisions were substantially subdued but never fully exorcised in the years when all Ukraine was within the USSR. Controversially, the republic's territory was expanded further by the transfer of Crimea from Russia under Khrushchev. This was a move which made some rough geographical sense, but no other sort, and was undertaken for reasons of internal political scheming. It was not popular with most of the people who lived in the peninsula, but made little practical difference in the context of a centralised Soviet Union. Throughout the post-war years Ukraine developed as a centre of Soviet industry and agriculture, and its leaders were prominently integrated into the overall Soviet leadership.

The dissolution of the USSR, undertaken at speed and with scant regard for likely ensuing nationality problems, created *de facto* a binational state in Ukraine, with a Ukrainian majority and a Russian minority mainly resident in the east and south of the country. This need not have been fatal to Ukraine's stability had it followed a democratic course of development. However, its oligarchic elites, from both sides of the national divide, instead embarked on a rapacious programme of self-enrichment. The economy collapsed and politicians became bywords for corruption.

Elections were generally pretty closely contested, tilting one way and another between groups with a pro-Russian orientation and those looking to tie Ukraine into the structures of the west. The latter ensured that Ukrainian troops took part in the occupation of Iraq. A fraudulent election allegedly won by Victor Yanukovych, an oligarchic tool from the east, was successfully challenged by mass street action. However, the pro-western leaders Yuschenko and Tymoshenko proved just as corrupt and inept. As a result, Yanukovych won the Presidency fair and square in 2010.

Maidan and beyond

Contrary to myth, Yanukovych was hardly a slavish sycophant of Putin. Rather, he pursued the interests of his own oligarchic bloc, not neglecting any opportunity for personal plunder. However, his political base lay in the Russian-speaking areas of the country. In the Donbas, he secured more than ninety per cent of the vote. Under his presidency, the tug-of-war over Ukraine's future reached a critical tipping point. In parallel, the Kiev government negotiated with the European Union over a trade agreement and with Putin over joining his putative Eurasian Economic Union, which sought to bring together much of the old USSR in a common economic space. Rebuffed in trying to proceed in both directions, which would have corresponded to both Ukraine's economic interests and its political stability, Yanukovych ultimately indicated he would sign with Moscow.

That triggered the Maidan uprising, since the Russian choice outraged both those Ukrainians seeking a long-term western orientation, and far-right Ukrainian nationalists motivated mainly by Russophobia. It also triggered sustained intervention by the EU and the USA to bring down the Yanukovych regime which, for all its depredations, had been democratically-elected. The prospect of "losing" Ukraine, six years after it has been promised NATO membership, was too much for Washington. The demonstrations in Kiev turned violent with heavy neo-nazi involvement, and dozens of demonstrators were shot. Who did the shooting remains somewhat obscure – regime forces, insurrectionists or both. In the chaos Yanukovych ultimately fled, and a new government was put together under US direction.

It could well be argued that this marked the real beginning of the Ukraine war. It certainly marked a step back for Ukrainian democracy and a definitive rupture in its delicate political-national balance. In the face of what was essentially a nationalist-NATO coup, Putin moved rapidly to seize control of Crimea, home to Russia's Black Sea Fleet. This was surely a breach of international law, like the forced separation of Kosovo from Serbia or the Turkish partition of Cyprus, but one that corresponded to the wishes of most of the people of the peninsula, who did not really want to be in Ukraine at all, still less under a nationalist-directed regime. It is not necessary to pretend that the referendum which ratified Crimea's transfer to the Russian Federation met the highest democratic standards to recognise that the Russian people of Crimea, the great majority of the population, supported the move.

The nationalist coup also triggered uprisings in the two major Russian-speaking regions in the east, Donetsk and Luhansk, together referred to as the Donbas. These areas had, as noted, been very strongly supportive of the ousted Yanukovych. Additionally, they were places were a strong pro-Soviet culture endured, to which the Ukrainian chauvinist posturing of the nationalists from the west of the country was deeply alienating. The movement there began as a popular uprising with a strong working-class component, before settling into a frozen conflict after Ukrainian government troops tried to over-run the region and were repulsed with Russian military assistance. Two "independent" regions were established, covering about a third of the territory of the two provinces. The governments there lost their popular character as they became dependent on Russia for their continued existence. Unlike in Crimea, whether the people there were content with the new arrangement is moot.

Agreements were hammered out between Russia and Ukraine, sponsored by France and Germany, at Minsk, under which Kiev would regain sovereignty and border control in return for giving the Donbas a broad autonomy of a sort not unusual in the constitutional arrangements of multinational states. That, however, was more than post-Maidan Ukraine could stomach, and the successive governments of Poroshenko and Zelensky failed to implement the Minsk agreements. Instead a low-level civil conflict rumbled on in the Donbas, costing 14,000 lives on all sides over the last eight years.

Ukraine's political culture scarcely improved during this time. Poroshenko, a wealthy oligarch and the immediate successor to Yanukovych, saw his support collapse amidst the usual welter of allegations of state and personal corruption. Nazi collaborators were overtly celebrated, and fascists entrenched themselves in the state apparatus, including establishing their own units within the armed forces. Those responsible for the 2014 massacre of anti-Maidan demonstrators in Odesa – 42 were immolated in a trade union building – went unpunished [5]. The Communist Party of Ukraine, once a powerful force in the country's post-1991 politics, was effectively banned. Russophobia has been given free rein, with curbs on the public use of the Russian language inter alia. It has become a foundation stone of the Ukrainian national identity shaped in the post—Soviet years. "Decommunisation" was used as a lever to humiliate all those proud of the collective Soviet past, something which had united many Ukrainians and Russians alike. Zelensky, a former TV comedian, was elected to succeed Poroshenko but made limited progress in securing Ukraine's democratic and economic development, or peace with Russia. Ukraine continues to stand out for its refusal to vote for United Nations resolutions condemning Nazism (a distinction it shares with the US alone).

The regime in place is not fascism, but neither is it democracy. Indeed, while the fascists have negligible electoral support, elections seem to determine relatively little in Ukraine and the far-right exercises a form of veto over aspects of government policy, including resolving the Donbas crisis. Certainly they have an extended cultural hegemony, as well as a state apparatus indulgent of their excesses. Should Zelensky cut an unwelcome deal with Russia to end the war, a further coup cannot be discounted.

There was nothing fore-ordained about Ukraine's riven, oligarch-raddled and fascist-infested state, more than thirty years after independence. Other multinational countries have negotiated such divisions better. The argument that its effective binational nature must mandate a division echoes the arguments of Ulster unionism, for example, with its insistence that a different national identity amongst the British-identifying community in north-east Ireland justifies separation. It is, to say the least, not obvious that the Russian-inclined east of Ukraine want the "self-determination" offered by Putin in any case. Russia's polity is scarcely attractive, nor its methods for extending assistance to its proclaimed kin. Only the people of Donbas, given a democratic opportunity for self-expression, can answer the question.

A democratic culture, building on the established ties of the Soviet period, could have given Ukraine better prospects. But a generation or more of oligarchic looting and clan politics beggared the country, economically and spiritually. Wartime vigilantism and bans on left-wing political activity do not betoken a much better future, however the war ends.

Return of Great Russia

One thing we can be sure Vladimir Putin is not trying to do with his war is recreate the Soviet Union, pace some of his western critics whose antipathy outstrips their political understanding and their rhetorical originality. If USSR 2.0 were his aim, he could start a good deal closer to home, by nationalising oligarchic property and prioritising the people's welfare. The Soviet Union was a social project, not simply an agglomeration of territory, and as such it was anathema to Putin and the layer in Russian society that he represents.

A further clue as to Putin's anti-Soviet orientation is that he keeps attacking the policies and the governing ideology of the Soviet time. Lenin and the Bolsheviks are scored for permitting the creation of a Ukraine (and other republics) and Stalin, a more serviceable leader from a Russian nationalist point of view, attacked for not renouncing self-determination as a principle. Whatever the Russian president is about, it is not socialism nor world revolution.

Rather, his 22 years at the helm of the Russian state represents the normalisation of the capitalist counter-revolution of the 1990s, the consolidation of the wild-west oligarchs of the Yeltsin period into a regular ruling class occupying a more stable relationship to the state pursuing their interests. Putin is one of Soviet power's executioners, not its putative restorer. Those who rightly protest Ukraine's nasty habit of memorialising Nazi collaborators, anti-Semites and mass executioners should also note Putin's proclivity for celebrating the life and works of the most barbarous White generals, not a whit better than the nationalist Ukrainians, from Russia's own civil wars. Likewise, no critique of Ukraine's democratic limitations can be undertaken without also acknowledging Russia's authoritarian system and Putin's dictatorial conduct, on show during the war in his suppression of the small but brave opposition to the invasion.

The marginal forces in Britain's anti-war movement championing Russia's conduct are in fact reluctant to attempt an analysis of the post-Soviet Russian state altogether, lest it render their support for the Putinist regime politically inexplicable. But a war has (at least) two sides and the regime in Russia demands scrutiny too.

Russia today is pre-eminently the product of the demise of the Soviet Union, consummated between 1989 and 1991. This first led to the replacement of the planned economy by commodity-money relations and then, once the Communist Party had been overthrown, by the privatisation of what was then the world's second largest economy, before it unravelled in a collapse of vertiginous and almost unbelievable scale.

This privatisation – which aimed more than anything else at creating a new capitalist class – proceeded along several lines. Some of the powerful, vertically-integrated industries were simply handed over to insiders by Yeltsin. Others became controlled by mushrooming private banks through a corrupt voucher privatisation scheme. A third avenue was installing private control over state revenue streams, creating openings for arbitrage and other forms of low-risk speculation. Newly-empowered regional leaders created their own politico-economic fiefdoms. At the peak of this structure sat a small and immensely rich and powerful oligarchy which both appropriated the Soviet peoples' wealth and came to control the apparatus of the state, bending the public power entirely to its will. The bombardment of the elected Russian parliament in 1993 and the rigging of Yeltsin's 1996 re-election as President (the Communist candidate was likely actually victorious) were landmarks in this degeneration. Rudi Dornbusch, a leading US economics professor, not unjustly said that the newly-minted capitalists had seized "wealth…created by corruption, theft and violence on a scale probably unprecedented in history." [6] They created a regime with medieval levels of inequality, which persists to this day.

This new capitalism therefore emerged with a high propensity towards monopolisation, just as Russian capitalism did first time around in the 1880s. There was no Adam Smith here, nor the slow development of monopoly capitalism which characterised industrial

Britain for example. Driven by the requirements of competition (in the domestic market as much as internationally) Russia's new rulers combined both backwardness, relative to the west, in respect of technique, with a high level of capital centralisation. As early as 1996 the US business press was describing the emerging structure of Russian industry as akin to South Korean chaebols – integrated conglomerates uniting financial and industrial interests in an almost-classic confirmation of the analysis of Lenin in his *Imperialism, the Highest Stage of Capitalism.*

This new elite was initially insecure in its purchase on Russian society – it had no roots, no mission beyond brazen gorging on misappropriated wealth. It craved only approval in the eyes of western imperialism, as well as homes in Knightsbridge and Upper West Side and yachts in the Mediterranean. As late as 2000 Putin was soliciting Bill Clinton to secure Russian entry into NATO. Russia did, for a time, join the G-8 top table of the "new world order." This was an attempt to secure an ersatz legitimacy which ultimately failed. Integrating a state and economy the size of the Russian into the existing institutions of international imperialist management would have compromised US hegemony, which preferred a super-imperialism in which it alone was the superpower to an ultra-imperialism which would see the clashing interests of the various great powers fused and transcended.

The US, not to forget the people of Ukraine, is now reaping the fury of a Russia scorned, of a Russian elite forced down the route of aggressive competition and expressing the great power traditions in its collective psyche. Bluntly, Putin and Russia were not taken seriously. The accommodation of US interests in central Asia by Russia after 9/11, for example, secured nothing for Moscow. Yet Putin's Russia was stabilised – more prosperous, in part due to high oil prices internationally, with the oligarchs placed in a more conventional relationship to the state, entrenched but obedient – and more ready to assert its own expanding interests.

The initial displays of this, however, had a reactive character if not exactly a defensive one. Russian troops moved into Georgia to defend the autonomous region of South Ossetia from an attempt by the Georgian government to subdue the Ossetians by force. The Ossetians have never had any desire to be governed as part of Georgia and Putin's move was far less an aggression than a support of their right to make their own choices – a clear example of a legacy conflict inherited from the hasty break-up of the USSR.[7]

We have already described the circumstances of Putin's next military deployment during the Ukrainian crisis of 2014. This was not a drama primarily of his making and, while it is fair to assume that Moscow held contingency plans for seizing the Crimea, it was the Maidan coup which prompted their implementation, and the part-secession of the Donbas, rather than any proactive step by a Russian regime which had still believed it could secure its interests in Ukraine politically prior to the nationalist seizure of power in Kiev.

Putin's 2015 intervention in Syria in support of the beleaguered Assad government bore a different stamp. There was no compelling Russian interest beyond maintaining a friendly regime in power and retaining access to the Russian navy's base at Tartarus. While lawful, it was simply another great power intervention in the Middle East, and in Syria in particular. Russia joined around a dozen other powers with fingers in the Syrian pie.

Whether or not this is a record of an imperialist power can become a rather scholastic question. Some conduct such an assessment on the basis of a tick-box exercise, ranking the various states under pre-cooked categories of varying relevance, rather than looking at the actual political economy of contemporary Russia. Lenin observed that in the most general terms, imperialism was monopoly capitalism and a "striving towards violence and reaction." It would seem that Putin's Russia qualifies on both counts. Imperialist or not, it is surely a far weaker power than the USA, let alone the large bloc Washington has consolidated around itself (with new impetus as a result of the 2022 war) and a source of far less aggression, bloodshed and general mischief in the world than the latter. But its backwardness does not preclude it from being imperialist - rather, in an environment where it must compete, it preconditions it. As with Tsarist Russia in the First World War, a relatively primitive capitalism with a high degree of monopolisation and significant military-political resources can sustain an expansive imperialism. And any capitalist Russia looking for such a sphere of expansion would turn first of all to its ex-Soviet neighbours, geographically proximate, historically enmeshed and economically connected as they are.

Enduring multipolarity

It has thus become Ukraine's tragedy to be the battleground in a proxy war between NATO, headed by the US, and Russia. In the course of the conflict, Ukraine's people may well have regained a powerful sense of their own agency but it has yet to become the determining factor. NATO's supreme objective is not merely drawing Ukraine into the orbit of the western powers, it is maintaining the "unipolar moment" – the unchallenged world hegemony of the US ushered in by the end of the (first) Cold War – as long as possible.

Defeating Russia, a militarily significant regional power sitting outside the US-led structures, would be a victory in that struggle, and a politically bracing one after the humiliation of US authority by the Taliban in Afghanistan. It would reassert the appearance of the US as global top dog. The real target of this would, however, be China. Unlike Russia, China is a first-rank economic power that is increasingly competitive politically and diplomatically with the US. Its military, while weaker than the forces at the Pentagon's disposal, is becoming an increasing factor too. The rise of China is the greater long-term challenge to a US-dominated world and the most significant earnest of a genuine multipolarity in world affairs.

A diminished Russia would weaken China too, given the political friendship between the two countries trumpeted by Putin and Chinese President Xi Jinping shortly before the invasion of Ukraine began. Such is the logic of the proxy warriors in the west at any event. China's interest is in developing a multipolar world bound together by mutually-agreeable principles rather than the overweening power of one state.

That multipolarity will likely end up being reinforced rather than undermined by the militarised US pushback against Putin. Like the Russian President, NATO strategists may find themselves dealing with unintended consequences. For it is one of the glaring revelations of the war that the NATO position is very much not supported by most of the often-invoked "international community."

It is true that positive support for Russia's invasion is almost non-existent among the world's states. Even China has made clear the importance of upholding Ukraine's territorial integrity. But lack of support is not the same thing as agreement to oppose. Those countries which have chosen to abstain on the matter include not only China but

India, Pakistan, South Africa, Saudi Arabia and many more. Together they constitute most of the world's population.

Active backers of Washington's sanctions-and-armaments pressure on Russia are even less numerous – essentially they are limited to the NATO powers themselves and the US's allies in the Asia-Pacific region: Japan, South Korea, Australia and little else. Even the far-right government of Brazil has shown no interest. One week's issue of *The Economist* spelt out the problem. On one page the headline – "why Russia wins a degree of sympathy in Africa and the Middle East"; turn over and it's "Why won't India's government condemn Vladimir Putin" while the China column states "Mr Xi places a bet on Russia -China's backing for Vladimir Putin's war is all about its contest with America".[8] So not much unipolarity in evidence.

There are many reasons for this. A gloomy column in the *Financial Times* headed "West rash to assume most of the world backs its stance on Russia" noted three – disdain for western hypocrisy, the fact that "western values" are not universal, and resentment at the effects of western sanctions, which often affect third parties disproportionately.[9]

Particular countries have been influenced by specific factors – memories of Soviet assistance in the anti-apartheid fight in South Africa, for example; or close military ties in the case of India. Economic and trade factors play a part. But general geopolitical considerations seem to underpin most of it. Another *FT* writer outlined that African countries remembered "the west's rapacious colonial history, its frequent hypocrisies and disastrous invasions of Iraq and Libya." [10] Iraq abstained in the vote at the United Nations citing "historical background" as well it might.

This is not just about history, however. To take one recent example, Russia and China released Covid-19 vaccines to poorer countries while the west hoarded supplies. Multipolarity works for much of the world. The unipolar period was not marked by peace, but rather by repeated US-led aggressions. Most countries have little investment in its prolongation.

Of course, that is only one side of the picture. The war has also strengthened NATO, whatever its ultimate outcome in Ukraine. Two long-neutral countries, Finland and Sweden, seem likely to join once Turkish objections are overcome, extending the potential zone of confrontation. NATO troops will more eastwards, into lands where they can confront Russia across the width of a border. NATO has been infused with new purpose too, using its revival to deploy more troops eastwards and reassert its unity and "values". Whether this will endure is another matter – already France, Germany and Italy are grouping themselves into a "peace party" seeking an early end to the conflict, while the US-British-East Europe axis champions war to the end. Nevertheless only Russia is on the other side of the new dividing line across Europe. Rather than the fresh security architecture Europe needs (and should have secured in 1991) the US will be holding a series of daggers at Russia's throat.

However, even in the US itself there are those who see getting re-embroiled in Europe's disputes as a distraction not just from the country's imposing domestic difficulties but from the supervening confrontation with China, which has increasingly been the focus of US power and diplomacy from Obama's presidency onwards. There is far less consensus amongst its allies over that.

More guns, less butter

The consolidation of NATO is just one negative consequence of Putin's war. It is a conflict which is enmeshed in capitalist competition from the start, refracted through state action, and it is likely to aggravate many features of world capitalism today. This is a war with an immediate global impact.

First, starvation. Russia's invasion and the sanctions imposed by NATO in response, have both helped provoke a global food crisis pushing millions into hunger. Particular countries have a high level of dependence on crops from Ukraine. For example, long-suffering Libya gets more than 40% of its wheat from there. Equally straitened Lebanon gets over seventy per cent. India secures over three-quarters of its sunflower oil from Ukraine too. The blockade of Ukraine's seaborne trade, over and above the direct disruption of agricultural production caused by military action, has imperilled those supplies. Ukraine's major port, Odesa, is doubly blocked – the Russian navy prevents anything leaving while Ukrainian mine-laying, aimed at disrupting any amphibious assault, stops anything getting in. Mariupol's port is entirely destroyed. The capacity to move grain out of Ukraine by alternative, overland routes, is limited. Rather cynically, Putin has offered to lift the blockade in return for sanctions relief, undermining the argument of those who pretend that sanctions alone and not the war was the cause of the food crisis.

At present last year's Ukrainian harvest is largely in storage, unable to leave the country, meaning there will be nowhere to store this year's crop when it is brought in from the fields – up to 30% of the country's farmland may be unplanted or unharvested for 2022. All this is having a devastating effect on food prices in some of the world's poorest countries. Western-imposed sanctions are also making it hard for some countries to purchase supplies from Russia, even countries which are not themselves party to the sanctions. The ripples reach wide. Pigs are being culled in Ireland, for example, because the price of fertiliser and animal feed is rocketing as the war squeezes supplies of key inputs.

Second, the driving up of energy costs. The major factor here is not supply disruption but sanctions on Russian oil, coal and gas. This is impacting on household bills already rising sharply across the continent, as energy markets are upended. Such is the dependence of some European economies on these supplies that imposing a complete cut off of Russian supplies has proved very hard to make stick. Whatever pain is being inflicted on Russian business seems to be mirrored by the pain felt by European consumers.

Third, the war is promoting a general "deglobalisation". It is hastening the incremental unpicking of the integrated capitalist world economy which had to a substantial extent developed in the two decades after the cold war. Disrupted first by the crash of 2008, exacerbated by the growth of Trump-style economic nationalism, directed towards China above all, and further strained by the pandemic; the Ukraine conflict threatens to dig the trenches still deeper. Two rival politico-economic blocs facing off, one Chinese-Russian led and the other centred on the USA is looking like a plausible future. Sanctions are already leading to a drop in world trade, despite most countries not applying them. The consolidation of such divisions presage further conflicts down the road.

Fourth, and in that context, currency wars are beginning. The US has long sought to weaponise the dollar's commanding position in the international economy to secure its strategic ends. Now that supremacy may be starting to slip – even before the war the dollar's share of global reserves had fallen from 71% at the start of the century to 59%. More governments are understanding the vulnerability of holding foreign currency reserves in dollars given Washington's willingness to take action against Russia on that front, even though acting on such a perception is far from straightforward.

The sanctions against Russia could prove a turning point. As the *Financial Times* put it: "…by explicitly weaponising the dollar in this way, the US and its allies risk provoking a backlash that could undermine the US currency and sunder the global financial system into rival blocks that could leave everyone worse off."[11] Bluntly, trust in the US is declining among significant economic powers around the world. The long-term probability is of dollar-denominated and Chinese-controlled international financial systems, representing both a further decline in US global hegemony and a step towards institutionalised conflict. Not for the first time, imperialism's actions to address an immediate crisis will end up undermining its own interests.

Fifth, there is a major boost to the arms industry. More billions are to be spent on weaponry, certainly at the expense of meeting social needs. The global arms manufacturers will benefit mightily. Military spending in the key powers is set to soar. Germany has here set the pace, pledging to allocate an additional one hundred billion dollars to bolstering its armed forces. Britain, it seems, will not be far behind, with talk of escalating the defence budget from two per cent to three per cent of GDP annually – a leap of more than thirty billion pounds. New combat jets, new drones, more tanks and artillery, all while the cost of living soars and the scars of austerity remain unhealed.

All this helps condition the new geopolitics and ensures that fresh wars are being incubated. To paraphrase Winston Churchill, the Ukraine war is no more than the end of the beginning. It is the moment of transition from a unipolar world of neo-colonial wars to a world of open great power clashes. Here is the challenge to the anti-war movement worldwide.

Britain in the World Order

Boris Johnson's government sits front and centre of the world crisis. It is perhaps the most belligerent among the major European powers. Johnson and Foreign Secretary Liz Truss have devoted their energies to snuffing out any possibility of an end to the Ukraine war and a peaceful resolution of the disputed issues. They have only to hear a rumour of negotiations to mobilise immediately against it. They are aligned with the hardest-line voices in Washington and in eastern Europe. Johnson has insisted that there is no point in negotiating with Putin, who Truss says must be completely defeated. "We will keep going further and faster to push Russia out of the whole of Ukraine," the Foreign Secretary said in April.[12]

The government is supported in this whole-heartedly by Keir Starmer, who is paid from the public purse to serve as Leader of the Opposition and should be offering refunds by now. His "opposition" is not directed at Tory war-mongering but at the Stop the War Coalition and those amongst his own backbench MPs alive enough to the realities of the situation to ascribe some responsibility to NATO. He has turned the House of Commons into a monolithic stanchion for war, muting dissenting voices on pain of exclusion. Starmer's sole concern is his own respectability as a loyal servant of the state.

This is a cynical as it is criminal. The fight-to-the-death party are not actually proposing fighting themselves. They stand ready to see Ukraine bled dry to serve their strategic purpose. President Zelensky himself seems to be wise to Johnson, Truss and Starmer. Who else can he have had in mind when he told *The Economist* that there is a camp in NATO who "don't mind a long war because it would mean exhausting Russia, even if it means the demise of Ukraine and comes at the cost of Ukrainian lives"?[13] He puts his finger on the problem – the explusion of Russian troops from Ukraine, even the land seized by this aggression, never mind Crimea, can likely not be achieved by Ukraine at all, and if so only at immense and protracted suffering and destruction.

For Zelensky, as he said in the same interview, "victory is being able to save as many lives as possible…because without this nothing would make sense. Our land is important, yes, but ultimately, it's just territory." He has also indicated that Ukrainian neutrality, with security guarantees, would be an acceptable outcome, with NATO membership foresworn. Such talk is anathema to Britain's political leadership, who instead look forward to a permanently weakened Russia and a new lease of life to the world order which has privileged British imperialism's alliance with the US superpower.

Base politics are at work. Johnson needs the Ukraine war to prolong his shameless and shambolic premiership, using the exigencies of international diplomacy to hold his multiplying Tory critics at bay. In a dramatic example of perverse incentives, the leader of the Scottish Conservatives, Douglas Ross has opined that the Prime Minister should remain at his post as long as the Ukraine war lasts. Liz Truss for her part is relishing the war as a chance to strut her sub-Thatcherite stuff to get to the front of the queue to succeed John son when he is finally driven out of Downing Street. Simon Jenkins summed it up well: "Johnson and Truss have not declared that a Ukrainian deal is for Zelensky and his people to decide. They want him to keep fighting for as long as it takes for Russia to be utterly defeated. They need a triumph in their proxy war. Meanwhile anyone who disagrees with them can be dismissed as a weakling, a coward or pro-Putin. That this conflict should be hijacked by Britain for a squalid forthcoming leadership contest is sickening."[14]

Jonathan Powell, who helped negotiate the Good Friday Agreement in Ireland as Tony Blair's chief of staff, agrees. "It is for the Ukrainians to decide when, whether and what to negotiate with the Russians. Our role is to help and support them in negotiations as we have in war, not to make things worse by letting bellicose rhetoric run away with us." Powell also urges expanding talks beyond the immediate disputes at issue to include "a serious discussion with Russia about new security arrangements in Europe, including a new conventional forces agreement, a new intermediate nuclear force agreement and a new relationship between NATO and Russia."[15]

A long opinion article in the *New York Times* also reported that, when the author had been in Ukraine "even staunch Ukrainian nationalists expressed views far more pragmatic than those that are now routine in America now. Talk of neutral status for Ukraine and internationally-monitored plebiscites in Donetsk and Luhansk has been jettisoned in favour of bombast and grandstanding." The Anglo-American policy of expanding the boundaries of the war "is not just declamatory extravagance. It is reckless. The risks hardly need to be stated."[16]

But apparently they do. Those risks include not just the lingering evisceration of Ukraine and its people but the expansion of the conflict to draw in other countries. Already, the US and Britain lead in flooding Ukraine with arms for the sole purpose of prolonging a conflict to bleed a rival dry. Already, the air is thick with warnings that nuclear weapons might be used. Already, troops are being readied for eastward deployment. Putin bears his share of the blame for this, of course. But so too do the war party making the running in London and Washington.

Certainly, Johnson-Truss diplomacy is not universally appreciated. An authoritative article in US magazine The Atlantic reported that Truss's "stark language is unlikely to go down well in Paris and Berlin, where Britain's hawkish stance toward Russia has been quietly criticized since the beginning of the conflict. According to some diplomats and officials I spoke with, Britain's position has made reaching a cease-fire more difficult, driving up the price of peace that will be paid for with Ukrainian blood, and all in a fairly see-through attempt to restore Britain's reputation after Brexit. Even within the U.K. government, officials have voiced concern to me that Truss's hawkishness is partly a political play to improve her standing ahead of any contest to succeed Johnson."[17]

Even in Washington, there is anxiety at the British government's performative aggression. "American officials have at times been annoyed with the tough talk from UK Prime Minister Boris Johnson and foreign secretary Liz Truss," the *Financial Times* reports.[18] Britain is world-leading only in purblind bellicosity.

But in outline, the issue of peace in Ukraine divides along the same lines as war in Iraq did in 2003. On one side, the USA, Britain and eastern Europe (Ukraine was itself a participant in the Iraq aggression). On the other, France, Germany and Italy. Beneath a superficial unity, the old worm of inter-imperialist intrigue and rivalry is burrowing away.

Nor is that only in relation to Ukraine. British policy spares no effort in promoting a new cold war globally, aligning closely with the USA, sometimes at the expense of other allies. The "golden age" of British-Chinese relations promoted by David Cameron has now long past. The first voyage of Britain's new aircraft carrier was to the Far East, whence no threat to Britain's security or well-being emanates, but where the US is demanding solidarity with its own bipartisan confrontation with rising Chinese power.

Extending the same folly, Johnson joined the USA and Australia in a new arms race in the Pacific, initialling the AUKUS pact in 2021 to upgrade Australia's submarine fleet with new nuclear-powered vessels. In the process, France was gazumped, its own deal with Australia unceremoniously scrapped. Confrontation with China is best conducted in English only, it seems.

The bipartisan war front in British politics does not serve the British people well either. Ten years of public sector austerity, fourteen of frozen real wage levels and two of a pandemic are now succeeded by a growing cost-of-living crisis. Bills for all the necessaries for survival are soaring, while the Bank of England tries to hold wage increases down, purportedly in order to eliminate the inflation it has allowed to soar unchecked but in reality to ensure that ordinary people bear the burden of solving the economic dislocation caused by capitalism.

Adding the consequences of war to this has made matters much worse. Sanctions are adding to the cost of food and fuel. The demands for a huge rise in arms spending will inevitably squeeze social priorities competing for state funds.

Labour will not point this out, preferring to echo the government's war policy in every particular, trying to outbid it where possible. It imagines that it is following a path to electoral success, when it is in fact the road to the cliff edge.

So it falls to the anti-war movement to do so.

Conclusion

The Ukrainian conflict has produced a war psychosis in Britain without recent precedent. Certainly none of the previous wars of this century have inspired a comparable politico-media manufactured hysteria. Despite the absence of British forces actually engaged in fighting – traditionally the focus for patriotic mobilisation of varying efficacy – the establishment has thrown its all at winning public support for Ukraine and for continuing confrontation with Russia.

There is nothing humanitarian in this – the same media and political elite effectively ignore the British-armed and financed war on Yemen being conducted by Saudi Arabia and the United Arab Emirates, a war which has claimed around 300,0000 lives and constitutes the world's greatest humanitarian crisis, according to the United Nations. Yet you will see no Yemeni flags in the shop windows on chi-chi high streets. Perhaps it is that Arab people dying from imperialist wars is no longer news. Dog bites man etc. Certainly, the racism of the greater response to "blonde, blue-eyed people" suffering has been explicit.

There is, however, a strong humanitarian impulse in the mass sympathy being expressed for the Ukrainian people. They support a people whose homes have been laid waste and lives turned upside down, when they have not been lost altogether, by Putin's aggression. But the same government which stokes up support for Zelensky does barely the grudging minimum to assist Ukrainians seeking refuge in Britain. Those wishing to host refugees have faced a maze of bureaucratic obstacles, unique in Europe. Even this, however, is better than the welcome facing refugees from other conflict zones, for whom a one-way ticket to Rwanda is all that is on offer.

The anti-war movement has, to coin a phrase, been tough on the war and tough on the causes of war. This distinguishes it from the fringe element who cannot let a word of criticism of Putin slip past their lips on the one hand, and the much larger body of opinion on the left and beyond which is reluctant to face the realities of NATO (and British) responsibility for the circumstances which have permitted this war to flower.

Yet leaving those realities unaddressed merely makes the future still more threatening, turning a possible future conflict into a near-certainty. The new cold war will surely turn hot if the present policies of NATO (read: US) military expansion and sustained confrontation with China and Russia are maintained. As noted at the start of this pamphlet, this is a point Stop the War has long made. The post-Cold War world has been one of the unipolar domination of imperialism, mainly US imperialism, with the British version prominent too, militarily, politically and financially. That is now challenged by rising centres of multipolar power – China at a global level, Russia and Iran regionally.

Averting war arising from these clash of interests cannot be left to the politicians, who are not covering themselves in glory. It is pre-eminently a matter for the people. At the time of the Iraq War's outbreak a US journalist noted that the world had two superpowers – the USA and mobilised public opinion. That was probably not entirely true then, and the distribution of world power is more complex now. However, the role of mass mobilisation remains critical. Indeed, in a time of parliamentary inanition it is more critical than ever.

A 2020 opinion poll showed that Stop the War was the most popular campaigning organisation amongst the membership of the Labour Party. Keir Starmer has driven many of those members out of the Party, but his work is no more than half-done. He has used the

Ukraine conflict to try and break that sympathetic connection between part of Labour's membership and representatives and the anti-war movement once and for all. There is only one reason why a politician should wish to disencumber himself of the influence of anti-war opinion – it is to have a freer hand to fight wars.

Starmer is set on the Blair path. His Labour is one of unqualified support for US power and its NATO instrument, just as previous Labour leaders supported the Empire, in office at least. His aim is to exorcise the spectre of Jeremy Corbyn's anti-imperialism, one of Corbyn's most striking original contributions to Labour politics. Starmer fears it not because it was unpopular but because it wasn't – remember the positive public response to Corbyn's speech after the terrible terrorist attack in Manchester during the 2017 election campaign, in which the Labour Leader said such atrocities showed the failure and negative consequences of the "war on terror" waged by Britain.

It cannot be said presently how the Ukraine conflict will play out. It may be fought for a long time, to the enormous detriment of the people of Ukraine first of all. The anti-war movement, unlike the Johnson-Starmer bloc, is for the earliest possible negotiated settlement between Ukraine and Russia, the end to US imperial designs in Europe and the creation of a new European security plan which can start to efface the causes of tension across the continent. We oppose British military deployments in Eastern Europe, and the proposed gigantic increases in arms spending, just as we oppose the AUKUS pact in the Pacific and other provocations directed at China and campaign for the elimination of nuclear weapons before such weapons eliminate us.

This is a programme which meets the interests of the British people, if not its ruling class. It needs to be argued for in the workplaces, in the communities and on the streets. It already has support within the trade unions and a broader sympathetic understanding, including amongst those who condemn Russia's aggression and salute Ukraine's resistance. People understand that our main enemy, however, is here at home – an elite which has connived in the creation of this crisis, is seeking to exploit it and will certainly reproduce it on a still greater scale if left unchecked. As that understanding deepens and is organised, it will find a parliamentary echo no doubt.

That is the aim of the Stop the War Coalition and of the socialist and anti-imperialist left. It is beyond the powers of the Starmers and the Masons to exorcise it, since it reflects the deepest desires of the majority of humanity in the present crisis.

End Russia's Invasion!
No NATO expansion!
Stop escalation of the war!
Ceasefire and negotiations now!

Notes

1. *Flashpoint: World War III* by Andrew Murray (London: 1997). "The splits among the Ukrainian people, reflecting different histories and culture, could provide any number of internal pretexts and possibilities for external intervention." p 160
2. *Empire and Ukraine* by Andrew Murray (Croydon: 2015)
3. *The National Question* by Rosa Luxemburg (New York: 1976) p 298
4. These events are dealt with in greater detail in *Empire and Ukraine* pp 55-60
5. The UN Human Rights office stated in 2016: "... The investigations into the violence have been affected by systemic institutional deficiencies and characterized by procedural irregularities, which appear to indicate an unwillingness to genuinely investigate and prosecute those responsible."
6. *Business Week*, April 15 1996
7. See *Empire and Ukraine* pp 114-131 for a detailed review of this episode.
8. *The Economist* 12 March 2022
9. Edward Luce in *Financial Times* 25 March 2022
10. 'This is no time for neutrality in Africa on Ukraine" by David Pilling, *Financial Times* 25 March 2022
11. 'Will there be a backlash against the dollar' *Financial Times* 8 April 2022
12. 'The return of geopolitics: Foreign Secretary's Mansion House speech at the Lord Mayor's 2022 Easter Banquet', www.gov.uk 27 April 2022
13. *The Economist* 2 April 2022
14. 'Liz Truss risks recklessly inflaming Ukraine's war to serve her own ambition' by Simon Jenkins, *The Guardian* 28 April 2022
15. 'A negotiation plan to help Ukraine avoid catastrophe" by Jonathan Powell, *Financial Times* 12 May 2022
16. 'America and its allies want to bleed Russia. They really shouldn't' by Tom Stevenson, *New York Times* 12 May 2022
17. 'We're not going to make that mistake again' by Tom McTague, *The Atlantic* 9 May 2022
18. 'What is America's end-game for the war in Ukraine?' by Felicia Schwartz and Amy Kazmin, *Financial Times* 29 May 2022.

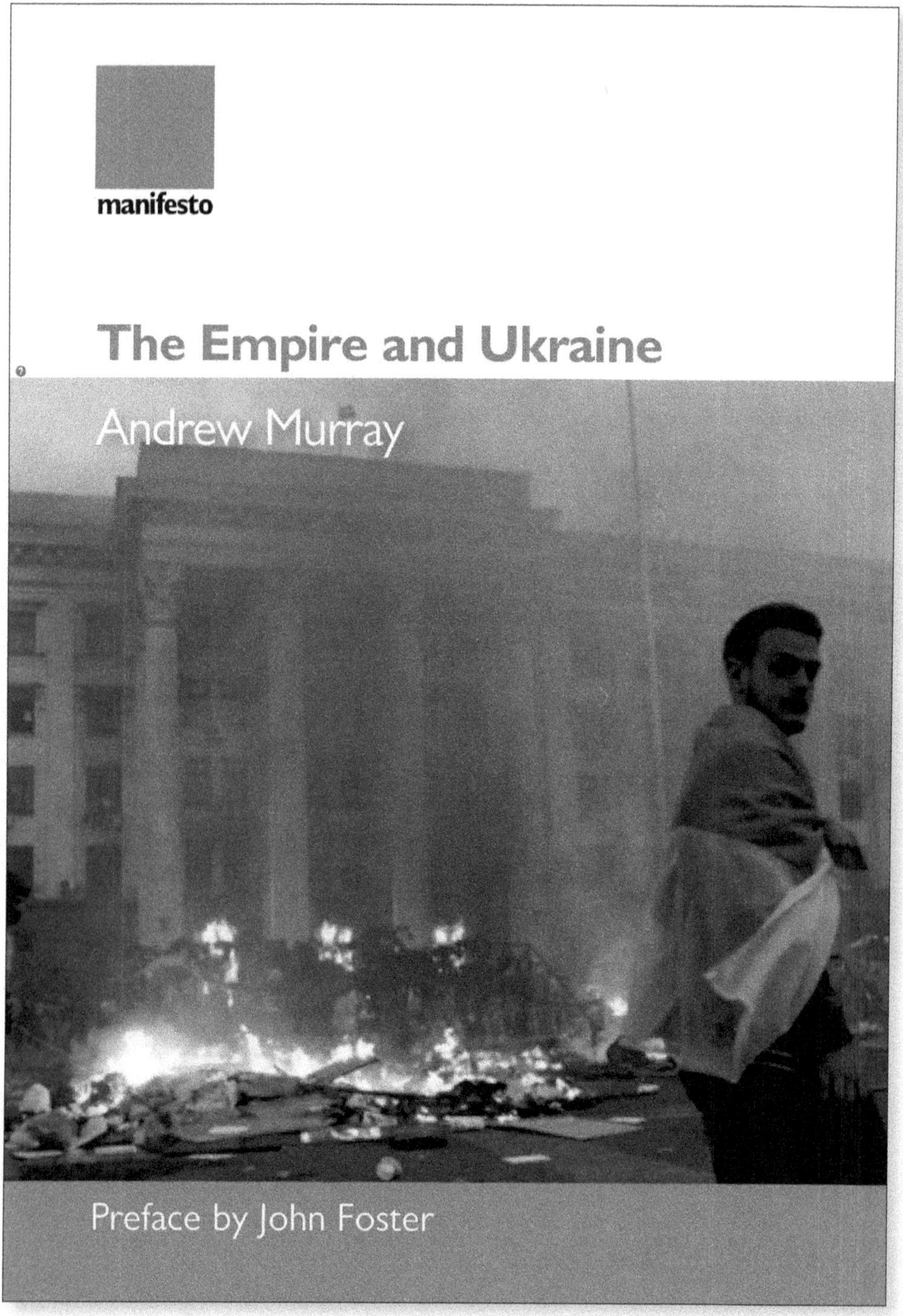

The Empire and Ukraine

Andrew Murray

Preface by John Foster

Preface to the 2015 edition John Foster

Andrew Murray has been a key figure in the British peace movement for the past two decades. As Chair of the Stop the War Coalition he helped mobilise the biggest anti-war demonstration this country has seen. Since the Iraq war, and indeed before, his writings have provided some of the sharpest exposures of the deceit and hypocrisy of those who wage war in the name of peace. More importantly, he has consistently sought to explain the origins of war and why aggression, whether economic or military, is integral to the type of exploitative society in which we live.

The Empire and Ukraine is therefore about far more than the current crisis in Ukraine. Murray uses the crisis to unravel the complex character of the relationship between the development of contemporary capitalism and the potentially lethal drive to military engagement that we have seen over the past two decades. Murray starts with Lenin's analysis of imperialism, written a century ago, and asks what has changed. Monopoly continues to generate super-profit. Big business and the banks continue to accumulate capital and struggle to find outlets for further investment. Dominant states still seek to service these economic imperatives. What has changed, argues Murray, is the configuration of states. This is what makes the world so dangerous today.

Unlike Lenin's world where half a dozen imperialist states vied for power, just one power, the US, was dominant for the half century after 1945 – only partially balanced by the Soviet Union. Since 1991 that balance has been removed but other states, notably but not only China, are now seen to be emerging as potential challengers. Capitalism as a system, says Murray, has also moved on. He disputes claims about total globalisation. But capital now operates in a far more globalised way and relies more on global institutions such as the World Trade Organisation, the IMF and the World Bank as well as NATO and the EU.

These developments now frame the actions of the United States as the dominant but declining super power. The Wolfowitz doctrine of 1992 outlined the long term US strategy. It is to ensure that in no segment of the world, the Far East, Europe, the Middle East, the Americas, does any other power become dominant and able to use that region as the basis for a wider challenge. In each region rival states must be balanced against each other and ultimately subordinate – and, if not, subdued by force. It is here that capital's new global institutions play a key role. All are ultimately dominated by the US and they act across capitalist states to mobilise 'multilateral' support for US strategies of regional dominance. Sometimes partially. Sometimes more fully. The brake that might otherwise be applied by rival, if lesser, powers is removed or weakened.

This is what makes the Ukraine crisis so dangerous. Murray demonstrates how Ukraine fits within the strategy for US regional dominance in Europe and specifically for the containment of Russia. He shows the role of NATO, the EU and the IMF in creating an 'international' consensus.

The Empire and Ukraine does many things. It provides new clarity on the development of Ukraine as a state. It details the country's Soviet heritage and why this is still a living reality for those in the east and south for those who want freedom from oligarch kleptocracy. It documents the unsavoury alliance of neo-liberals and fascists that currently hold the levers of power in Kiev. And, as with any writing by Murray, it provides searing polemic against those on the right and left who provide cover for intervention. But, most important of all, it analyses. Today, as the Labour Movement debates the role of the EU and NATO, it exposes the nature of actual existing imperialism, its drive to confrontation and how these 'international' organisations provide the soothing external rationale for war.

Introduction to the 2015 edition

THE WAR CRISIS which has gripped Europe in the wake of the events in Ukraine over the last two years has been nothing if not foreseeable. The present author wrote about the dangers nearly twenty years ago:

> "The Ukraine itself is clearly pregnant with the possibility of conflict, divided between a Russian-oriented and heavily industrial east, and a nationalistic west... .Russia's conflict with the Ukraine over control of the Crimea, most of whose people wish to be reattached to the Russian Federation, is a further source of friction. The US and Germany have clearly declared for an independent Ukraine, primarily as a means of weakening their Russian rival. Germany is in the lead here, too. It has established a council for the deepening of economic relations with the Ukraine, and the burgeoning Ukrainian fascist movement is closely aligned with German sympathisers." [1]

And: "Of all the new 'nation states' the Ukraine holds the greatest possibility for dramatic fragmentation....Russia cannot accept Ukrainian independence, still less its incorporation into a German bloc, without accepting its own permanent relegation to the second rank of powers and denying its privatised giant industrial companies the most obvious external market to attach. Yet without the Ukraine, Germany's domination of Europe would remain attenuated and provisional, always at the mercy of a Russian resurgence. The splits amongst the Ukrainian people, reflecting different histories and culture, could provide any number of internal pretexts and possibilities for external intervention." [2]

In 1997, when these prophecies appeared, few people either on the left or anywhere else were much interested in listening. The 1990s were the heyday of the "new world order" with its promise of a peaceful world benignly policed by US power. Conflict was to be confined to tidying up operations, dealing with the detritus of humanity's history in a post-historical world.

It is now of course banal to ridicule those sentiments, as well as poor Francis Fukuyama who expressed them in the most philosophically-rigorous form. The Yugoslav, Afghan, Iraq and Libyan wars are all behind us. The "no more boom and bust" globalised capitalism of the post-Soviet world has...bust. We were not interested in war and crisis but, as it turned out, war and crisis were very much interested in us.

Today, a barely-supressed civil war is being fought in Ukraine; Russia aligning with one side, and NATO, the USA and the European Union with the other. On the other side of the world, the great powers of the Pacific – and some lesser ones too – manoeuvre against each other and issue competing aggressive declarations.

How are we to understand this? Last year, the 100th anniversary of the outbreak of the First World War was marked, complete with speculation about a repetition. In 2016 the battle of the Somme, along with Verdun the emblematic carnage of the whole conflict, will get its centenary in turn, and the year after that the great revolution in Russia. These historical events to some extent frame our conception of the present crises. For example, the anniversary of the First World War has brought the issue of imperialism to the fore once more. That this catastrophic conflict was caused by imperialism and its rivalries is far from being an historical consensus, but it is fairly mainstream in one variation or another, and is far from confined to the Marxist left, whatever former Education Secretary Michael Gove may have asserted in his polemics against *Blackadder* histories of that war. Many people have wondered, with quite some justification, as to whether we may not be dealing with that imperialism once more, one hundred years on, as the system transitions from neo-colonial wars in Iraq and Afghanistan to the prospect of still bigger conflicts in Eastern Europe or the South China Sea.

The passages quoted earlier come from the author's 1997 book warning of the recrudescence of inter-imperialist rivalry in the "new world order". The basic theme seems to have been endorsed by the passage of time, notwithstanding various weakness in analysis and assessment, including the overestimation of the relative decline in US power (or a failure to anticipate the cosmetic masking of that decline by the whirlwind of financial speculation which ended in 2008). It also rather ducked the question of the nature of rising Chinese power (it has since risen a good deal further) and what this might mean for international politics.

However, it was correct in pinpointing the possibility of a major international conflict arising from the Ukrainian "flashpoint". So it has happened, and largely for the reasons cited in the passages above. The "Ukraine question" is now at the centre of world politics. On the international plane the Ukraine is the most important dispute in what is often called a revived "Cold War", as EU-NATO's continual post-1991 eastward advance has met Russian pushback. A wide range of economic sanctions have been imposed by the G7 states and their allies on Russia, while the latter increasingly aligns with China and other non-US allies in a putative attempt to create a new pole of global power.

So far, so bad. But worse could yet be to come. Many in official Washington (and London and Paris) are calling for a still stronger NATO response to the Ukraine crisis. It is probable that they will have an even greater influence on the next US administration than on the Obama one. NATO troops and heavy weaponry are moving east, into Poland and former republics of the Soviet Union itself. More than 20,000 troops took part in NATO military exercises in the first half of 2015 alone, along with 49 warships and 40 aircraft, including nuclear bombers. Provocative military demonstrations have bene held in Nerva, a Russian-populated district of Estonia right on the border with Russia. Naval war games have been conducted by NATO from the Black Sea to the Baltic. Atlanticist strategists are already talking of "Britain's mothers having to see their sons shed blood on the Latvian border". Russia is also holding large-scale exercises, albeit on its own territory, and its air force is expanding its range of operations across Europe. It is hardly hyperbole to see in the great power clash over Ukraine the outlines of a new world war. Indeed, in August 2015 the European Leadership Network think-tank warned that the competing Russian and NATO military manoeuvres were making a real war more likely. Helpfully, no less a strategist than Prince Charles has described President Putin as a new Hitler, and we all know how that ended (given his family support for the actual Hitler in the 1930s, complete with pictures of his Granny giving the Nazi salute, one might have thought that Princely discretion would have bene a wiser option). This is not a conflict European public opinion sees as necessary. A continent-wide poll shows a great reluctance to confront Russia militarily. But that is barely slowing the NATO moves. [3]

This book examines the Ukraine crisis – how it has arisen and why – while also using it is a starting point to view contemporary world politics. There are any number of works describing what has happened in Ukraine, some will be discussed here. The purpose of this one is to set the crisis in a more general context of post-1991 world politics, and to outline how the political left, the labour movement and anti-war campaigns should respond to it. We therefore have to integrate various perspectives, including setting a global context, to endeavour to come to that understanding.

First, the perspective of international relations – the crisis has in large measure been provoked by the continuing drive eastward in Europe by the USA and the European Union, the main props and beneficiaries of the post-1991 "new world order". It is often said, and rightly, that the "unipolar moment" of unchallenged US world domination is passing; nevertheless US power, abetted in this case by the EU, is best seen as undermined and in relative decline, but it remains the only contender for a global hegemonic role. Even as it is troubled in the Middle East, and "pivoting" its immense military resources to the Far East to contain and confront ascendant China, it still looks to incorporate other countries within its zones of control (influence is too kind a word), that is to say the formal and informal structures of the "New World Order". That does not mean that in Ukraine, any more than in Iraq, this a matter of having to introduce capitalism – capitalism already exists in the Ukraine, and has done for a generation. Instead, the aim is to remove regimes that stand outside of and opposed to the US/EU order, that might fall under the sway of other emerging powers (in this case Russia, obviously), or that may challenge the norms of the US-directed "international community", and the economics of the "Washington Consensus" by simple failure to conform to them. That expansionism by western imperialism (a term we will examine), directed at the Ukraine over many years, seeking to incorporate the country's considerable economic potential and resources within the orbit of the EU and NATO, was clearly a trigger for the present crisis.

The international relations perspective also includes the revival of Russian power, as a potential rival to the USA. Russia suffered a humiliation and collapse after 1991 on a scale which is normally associated only with losing a major war. Industrial production was halved, the social infrastructure was degraded and pushed back generations, and the partition of the USSR along the lines of its internal republican boundaries left millions of people in "the wrong country", that is to say in states which they felt no necessary allegiance to. These millions were mainly, but far from entirely, Russians living outside the Russian Federation itself. To these ethnic and national ties can be added powerful economic connections, reflecting the integrated nature of the Soviet economy, now fragmented into fifteen separate state economies and at the same time transferred to capitalist ownership and control. The inevitable gradual reassertion of Russian power has further stimulated the instability inherent in this situation. There is little to admire in Putin and Putinism – he presides over an authoritarian regime run mainly in the interests of the oligarchic groups which have seized the wealth of the USSR. It is a brazenly corrupt system, which has concocted an ideology mixing Russian chauvinism and Orthodox-influenced social conservatism, a mixture which holds almost no international appeal (unlike Communism, it should be added), to give it some appearance of purpose and popular base. Russia is also clearly a capitalist great power which would very much like to be admitted to the circle of world powers, even under US leadership. It was happy to be included in the G8 summits while it was on the invite list. There is a debate, which can be a bit scholastic in view of the above agreed facts, as to whether contemporary Russia is "imperialist" or merely reactionary and capitalist. Nevertheless, that too is addressed, as much for its long-term importance as for its bearing on the present situation in Ukraine. What is more important perhaps is to recognise the two-sided process driving Russian involvement in Ukraine – the support given by Moscow to entirely legitimate democratic and national demands by the Russian or Russophone people of the country, and the certainty that Putin's own motivations are strategic and economic, promoting the interests of his domestic oligarchy, more than they are democratic.

The first part of this book examines questions relating to the international setting – the nature of contemporary imperialism, the role of NATO and the European Union in general, the place of Britain in the world order and the impact of the economic crisis that began in 2008 on world politics – and how they relate to Ukraine. It endeavours to form a view of the specific nature of the world system today, utilising but not bound by Lenin's famous analysis of 100 years ago. The road to the Ukraine crisis lies through the dynamics of contemporary imperialism and its institutions.

Second, there is the perspective of Ukraine itself. This requires a brief history of the Ukrainian nation and state, in Soviet times and since. The conflict which began to erupt at the end of 2013 is rooted in Ukrainian as well as international realities of course, in particular different beliefs on what it means to be Ukrainian and what Ukraine should be, in turn drawing not just on more distant history but on the spectacular failure of the post-Soviet Ukrainian state to offer prosperity, democracy or a clear sense of identity to its people. Ukraine today presents a grotesque picture. In the last two years it has seen an elected, if corrupt, President ousted from office amidst violent demonstrations; one of its provinces annexed by Russia and a further two become the epicentre of a rolling civil war costing thousands of lives; beyond those centres of conflict, there has been at least one uninvestigated massacre which killed forty-eight people (a minimum official figure) in Odessa and the economy has, after years of oligarch-dominated stagnation gone into a neo-liberal prescribed freefall instead. The civil war in two of its eastern provinces has been barely patched over by a very shaky "truce" and looks liable to re-erupt at any moment – indeed, such a development seems almost inevitable. The new central government in Kiev, initially propelled to power in a western-backed coup against an elected President, is increasingly being taken over by a coterie of US-sponsored neo-liberals, IMF apparatchiks and neo-conservatives.

Many of them, strangely for a supposedly nationalist government, turn out not even to be Ukrainian, the appointment of former Georgian President Mikhail Saakashvilli as Governor of the divided province of Odessa being only the most egregious example. A large number of politicians associated with ex-President Yanukovych's Party of the Regions have apparently committed suicides which, on closer inspection under pressure, turn out not to be suicides at all. And of course the Kiev government has, despite international academic protests not only banned any description of the USSR as other than a criminal regime, but has also criminalised any criticism of Hitler's Ukrainian collaborators, a unique development. The popularity of the government is plummeting, according to all opinion polling. It is not a regime which is going to bring peace and harmony to its peoples any time soon.[4]

The second part of the book relates, in very summary form, the historical background to the emergence of the 2013-14 crisis in Ukraine and looks at the political and social forces which have emerged since, as well as outlining different international views on the conflict.

Finally, there is the perspective of political action. How should the working-class movement, and the anti-war campaigns, assess and respond to the events in Ukraine, and thereby in turn shape them? There is no sign that public opinion in most western countries wants to go to war against Russia in the cause of NATO enlargement. As recent history shows, however, that is not enough. Few people are as yet fully aware of the real dangers building up in the East and many, of course, are influenced by the "plucky little Ukraine" narrative being spun by NATO propaganda, which pits a unified democratic Ukraine against a revanchist Russia. It is yet to be clearly understood that the forces and ideologies behind external intervention in the conflict in Eastern Europe bear a close resemblance to those which have laid the Middle East to waste in the course of this century. [5]

The final section discusses various left responses to the Ukrainian issue in a more polemical form, and is supplemented by a selection of writings which appeared as the crisis was unfolding in the first half of 2014, since they underline and develop various points made in the text. As a further appendix, an article written in response to the Georgian war of 2008 is included, since both the event itself and the arguments in connection with it prefigured much done and said around Ukraine six years later.

This volume cannot definitively answer all the questions arising from this war crisis. It is at the mercy of events, which could speedily overtake any provisional conclusions reached. However, reasserting the connection between imperialism and war, a lesson which cannot be repeated too often alas, and the importance of opposing the inherent drive to inter-state conflict built into the DNA of the prevailing world order, is a message which will not become redundant until political action makes it so.

Perhaps there is little to add to the insight of the Neapolitan scholar Lorenzo Valla concerning the origins of war. As long ago as 1440 he itemised the causes as "desire of glory", "hope of booty", "fear of incurring disaster later, if the strength of others were allowed to increase" and "avenging a wrong and defending friends". All of these elements appear to have played a part in the decision of George Bush to attack Iraq in 2003, from access to oil, strategic advantage and anger at the attempted assassination of his father by Saddam Hussein. They also loom large in the US approach to the Ukraine today – booty is there to be had, the accruing strength of Russia could lead to a disaster, and there are friends (clients might be a better term) to be defended. A writer reviewing Valla's work in the early 17th century argued that he should have added religion to his list of causus belli. And that too has featured – in the form of attacks on Islam – in the explanations for some of today's wars. Slightly recast as the famous "clash of civilisations", with the west confronting Asiatic and Orthodox Muscovy in the interests of European enlightenment, it stalks 21st century Europe too. [6]

NOTES

1 Murray 1997, p 49
2 *ibid*. p 159
3 *Guardian, Financial Times*, both August 12 2015
4 poll reported in *Financial Times* August 1/2 2015
5 poll in *Financial Times* June 10 2015
6 Hale pp. 108, 127

PART ONE
21st Century Imperialism

HERACLITUS (535-475 BC) is credited with originally coining the phrase "nothing is constant except change". It has worn well ever since, although this has not stopped many people trying to make exceptions. It is now one hundred years since Lenin wrote his celebrated pamphlet Imperialism, the Highest Stage of Capitalism as the First World War raged around him. He located imperialism in the developments which had transformed capitalism over the preceding generation. In particular, he listed five factors which he saw as defining the new epoch – the formation of finance capital, based on the increasing role of the banks; the development of monopolies in place of free competition in most key branches of industry; the export of capital from the metropolitan centres of capitalism to the colonies and other less developed markets; the division of the world market between these monopolies; and the division of the world itself into formal and informal empires under the hegemony of one or other of the great powers. All this was oriented towards raising the rate of profit for capital investment beyond what traditional "free enterprise" could now yield. He drew critically on the work of other Marxists, like Rudolf Hilferding and Nikolai Bukharin, as well as non-Marxists like, famously, the English Liberal J.A. Hobson who had written a pioneering work on the subject earlier in the century. The question of colonies and imperialism had also been widely debated in the Second International and many of its member parties in the period before the outbreak of war. Lenin's pamphlet became a textbook on the matter (one of the most influential political works of the twentieth century in fact), largely because his arguments fitted the facts of the age, and in part because by the time it came to mass attention Lenin had the authority of having lead the world's first socialist revolution behind him. When he concluded his preface to the French and German editions of the book, published in 1920, with the ringing declaration that "imperialism is the eve of the social revolution of the proletariat – this has been confirmed since 1917 on a world-wide scale," who would have been disposed to argue?[1]

Ignoring Heraclitus, many Leninists have treated this analysis as a dogma, as if imperialism one hundred years on aligns in every respect with the imperialism Lenin studied (itself clearly different from the colonial imperialism of the 18th century, of course, not to mention the imperialism of Ancient Rome). Those of different political positions also take their definition of imperialism from a point in the past, even if it is not 1916, and then declare it either non-existent today (because nothing now overtly resembles, say, the Congress of Berlin), or extant and unchanged because today's world can still just about be squeezed or stretched on a political Procrustean bed to appear to fit the contours of the past. Thus it is asserted that imperialism must be based on the possession of colonies, or at least an explicit semi-formal neo-colonial sphere of control; in which case the concept is really a matter for historians only. Or it embraces any state which bullies its neighbours or interferes in a self-interested way in the affairs of others – here Iran, Saudi Arabia, Rwanda, Pakistan and many others might be dragged within the tent. A variation, beloved of neo-conservatives, sees imperialism today as the world policy of bad regimes (Russia above all) but not of those who throw their weight about for the right reasons – the USA, obviously. They deny the possibility of a "democratic" power behaving imperialistically, despite the weight of contrary historical evidence. On the Marxist left, at least outside academia, the most common approach has been to stick with Lenin's celebrated five criteria, prove they are still operative to some extent or other and then proceed as if nothing much had changed.

Of course, even at the time Lenin's short work could not encompass every nuance to be explored on so central an issue, and it might be said that his description of finance capital described the contemporary German economy better than the British. Clearly the relative weight to be given to the factors he placed at the centre of his analysis varied from one imperial power to another. The export of capital, for example, played a central part in British imperialism but a more limited one, in the formal sense at least, in the Russian Empire. Lenin's aim was sharply and deliberately focussed on analysing the route to the war then burning all around. It is unlikely he intended it to be the last word on a subject as complex, challenging and changing as imperialism and world economy.

It has been argued, moreover, that the famous title of Lenin's pamphlet was the product of a mistranslation which gave Lenin's assessment of the subject an unintended millennial tinge, and that actually "the most recent", as in latest, rather than "highest" as in final, might have reflected his thinking better. In fact, Lenin was quite prepared to drop the word "imperialism" itself from the title altogether if that would help get the work past the censor. It could have appeared as Special Features of Recent Capitalism. Had it done so it might have made it easier for Lenin's followers to examine the changes in capitalism over the succeeding decades without having to cram any new developments into the same "highest" stage, which could only be followed by socialism. [2]

But there are important ways in which the title, however arrived at, was true to the work's essence. Lenin described imperialism as monopoly capitalism in a moribund and parasitic condition, incapable of self-renewal and, moreover, as having prepared all the economic ground for socialisation. Imperialism "…drags the capitalists, against their will and consciousness, into some sort of new social order, a transitional one from complete free competition to completer socialisation." A final stage indeed. In fact, capitalism has reconstituted itself several times on the basis of imperialism since Lenin wrote, with enduring common features to be sure, but radically enough to make the perception of it as "moribund" a century ago clearly outdated. As Marx wrote in *The Poverty of Philosophy* in 1847 "in practical life we find not only competition, monopoly and the antithesis of the two, which is not a formula but a movement. Monopoly produces competition, competition produces monopoly. Monopolists compete among themselves; competitors become monopolists…and the more the mass of proletarians grows as against the monopolists of one nation, the more desperate competition becomes between the monopolists of different nations. The synthesis is such that monopoly can only maintain itself by continually entering into the struggle of competition." So it has proved. The "pre-socialisation of production" has indeed been reproduced, on a far more extensive scale than in 1916, as monopolies have risen, fallen and risen again, first on a spatially narrower basis and then, today, on a still broader one, but the social revolution of the proletariat has been and gone – for now, at least - in half of Europe and never yet dawned in the other, more developed half. [3]

On the other hand, Lenin's analysis, in "ordinary human language", that the development of capitalism had arrived at a stage "when, although commodity production still 'reigns' and continues to be regarded as the basis of economic life, it has in reality been undermined and the bulk of the profits go to the 'geniuses' of financial manipulation" has seldom rung truer than today. Likewise the development of the rentier as a typical representative of the imperialist class, an idea Lenin developed from Hobson, has reached a still greater luxuriance. Today, the investor trumps the producer in the hierarchy of capitalist order at almost every turn and rentiers, making nothing but money itself, are the pillars of elite society. [4]

Between the various criteria characterising the new imperialism of a century ago and the anticipated socialist revolution, Lenin placed a single transitional factor, a hinge to open the door from the one to the other – uneven development. This posited that the technical development of the forces of production took place at different rates in the different capitalist states, giving the monopolies of certain countries what would normally constitute a competitive advantage over those of others. This, however, came up against the existing division of markets between corporations and cartels and indeed the division of the world's territory between rival formal and informal empires. Put simply, the most technically advanced economies did not control the most land, labour, markets or materials. This was the well-spring of war, whatever transient disputes may appear to spark a particular conflict, given the incapacity of the capitalists of the world to redistribute markets and resources peaceably in line with their relative strength. In this, Lenin differed not only from Kautsky, who foresaw a world of peaceful ultra-imperialism, but also Bukharin who theorised the development of an "organised capitalism" emerging from the state-directed war economy. Lenin instead emphasised, criticising Bukharin, that imperialism could not entirely reshape capitalism since it was "incapable of eliminating exchange, the market, competition and crises". [5]

This analysis critically informs world politics today. However, Imperialism is in need of a reassessment one hundred years on. It did not prove to be the eve of the social revolution of the proletariat after all, although the course history took was scarcely less dramatic. Of course, any re-evaluation can risk an abstruse and pedantic aspect. Many people now recognise imperialism when it manifests in the most brazen forms - the Anglo-American invasion of Iraq, for example. And the term has come back into current usage over the last dozen years or so – that is, it is no longer the exclusive preserve of the left, with its own codes and jargon – because it seemed to fit pretty well the post-9/11 policy of George Bush and Tony Blair. Some right-wing and liberal columnists and thinkers were calling for a new colonialism or imperialism to address the problems of several parts of the world even before the official kick-off of the "war on terror" in 2001. They have continued to do so, albeit slightly more sotto voce post-Iraq War. Robert Kagan, for example, one of the intellectual progenitors of that conflict, was particularly energetic along this line and remains so to this day. His articles urging that the US place itself at the head of a new imperialism appear regularly in learned journals in the USA – in preparation, no doubt, for what he hopes may be a new administration taking office in 2017, more amenable to his projects. [6]

Not all advocacy of imperialism, nor even its practice, is so in-your-face and shameless. Today it often calls itself "globalisation", and it fights wars to "spread freedom and democracy". So it may be useful to return to basics.

"Imperialism today may be said to display itself in coercion exerted abroad, by one means or another, to extort profits above what simple commercial exchange can procure" wrote British Marxist historian Victor Kiernan. It is a better definition than most, having the merits of simplicity and inner unity, connecting the role of the state with the requirements of private capital accumulation, and the centres of global economic power with the rest of the world. It is true to the essence of the Leninist analysis, putting the search for super-profit front and centre, without boxing it into Lenin's specific five-point imperial criteria. [7]

So how does super-profit extorted by coercion work today, and does "abroad" have any real meaning anymore? Capitalist globalisation is surely one of the new circumstances, and one of the most important in the twenty-first century. There is a sense in which globalisation has changed very little at least from a longer view of human development. Lenin, in his booklet on imperialism, cited the work of contemporary German economist R. Calwer, who had divided the world into five "main economic areas" – Europe excepting Russia and Britain; Britain; Russia; the Far East; and America. The main significant change in the distribution of world power between then and today has been the partial and contested absorption of Britain into a bloc with the USA, on the one hand, and Europe on the other, while still trying to play an independent role. And, yes imperialism is still "an immense accumulation of money capital in a few countries". [8]

Imperialism has also, in its manifold forms, always presented itself as a solution to the problem of surplus capital, to the difficulty in finding continuing investment opportunities in a "domestic" market, however defined, without precipitating a fall in the rate of profit. Such a fall need not be alarming, still less catastrophic, in the short term, particularly if the mass of profit holds up, but over a longer-run it compromises the capacity of businesses to capitalise surplus value and continue with unimpeded accumulation. In its earlier colonial phase, centring on the export of capital by banks and monopoly combines, imperialism addressed the profit problem by investing in countries where the colonial exploitation of labour yielded a far higher rate of surplus value particularly in the production, processing and transportation of raw materials, critical to the formation of constant capital.

Capitalist globalisation, enforced by economic and if needs be extra-economic coercion wherever it hits barriers, has both extended and complicated the opportunities for investment and accumulation. It is in this sense a new phase of imperialism. The mechanisms are modified, although control of cheap production resources remains critical. Technological rents and the varied forms of financial exploitation have ascended in significance as mechanisms of control by the imperial centres of world economy. These have not, however, changed the underlying tendencies towards over-accumulation of capital, whether that is expressed in conventional crises of over-production (or commodities) of the bubbles of the last twenty years, culminating in the collapse of the great credit bubble in 2008. Nor have they changed capital's continuing requirement for a lack of homogeneity in the world economy, that is areas (spatial or sectoral) where surplus capital can be invested at a rate that generates a "super-profit", even as the development of globalisation tends towards a levelling-out of the world economy and a reduction of national differences – including ultimately divergences in the rate of profit, which in any given circuit of accumulation tends towards equalisation. This contradiction is by no means a critical one in the short term, when the new globalised capitalism is on the ascendant, drawing in vast new supplies of wage labour and opening up more and more markets, but in the present slump it can become acute. How to reproduce opportunities for super-profit while bubbles are bursting all around and a variety of regimes with a range of motivations and ideological inspirations are challenging the hegemonic world order?

Certainly, globalisation has put to bed through practice the theory associated above all with Karl Kautsky that worldwide capitalist integration would be associated with a policy of peace. The war policies of Bush and Blair instead exhibited in full luxuriance the policies (conquest of other nations), the motivations (strategic, commercial) and the moralising (evangelical humanitarianism) long associated with imperialism in its more "liberal" presentations. The similarities with the world before 1914 are certainly significant – but so too are the differences. In so far as today's imperialism remains an imperialism of nation-states (and to a very large extent it does) it appears an imperialism of the USA above all; a state that has reached a degree of relative power which, even as it slips from its pinnacle, is far greater than any state could attain, or even hope to, in 1914 (or 1939 for that matter). To the extent that economic globalisation and its more limited parallel political institutions, allied to the unprecedented ascendancy of one state, have made contemporary imperialism not one of nation-states new issues arise. Greek economist – and presently an MP for the Syriza breakaway – Costas Lapavitsas argues, for example, that "formal imperialism has become practically irrelevant in contemporary capitalism, but mature capitalist countries have retained a dominant role in economic activity across the world", with financialisation now the main means of integrating the world economy under their hegemony. The aggressive use of tariffs, the absence of exclusive territorial control and the generalisation of capital export, often in the reverse direction to that of 100 years ago (i.e. from 'developing' countries to 'developed') are other differences he draws attention to. [9]

If monopolies seek to redivide markets not through the agency of support from "their" nation-states but through multilateral institutions, if the struggle for "spheres of influence" no longer takes a zero-sum form where it exists at all, then to what extent are we any longer discussing the same imperialism as prevailed from the 1880s or so until 1945? And if the export of capital becomes not a special feature of capitalism in its strongholds, but a pervasive norm of the globalised economic system with all capital increasingly disrespectful of state frontiers – when "abroad" is, for capital, everywhere and hence nowhere - what value do we now place on its export as a driver of political imperialism? What indeed does "export" even mean here, when globe-girdling banks have concentrated vast sums in their hands? What validity does Lenin's idea of uneven development have today, in short, when the equalising factors between the major powers are so much stronger than they were?

These questions put front and centre the issue as to what sort of imperialism we have in the world today – capitalist, certainly, but that does not say enough – and how this shapes international politics, including the crisis in and over Ukraine. This is not an abstruse, or angels-on-a-pinhead, point. The nature of the imperialist world system today, or our assessment of it, directly informs our political choices. If all the great powers are much of a muchness, then there is no particular reason to single out the depredations of the USA and its allies for special attention. Of course the enemy would, in the spirt of Karl Liebknecht, still be "at home", but the Ukraine could be presented as a tussle between two equivalent imperialist groups, US-led and Russian, which should be treated as equal menaces to the peace of the world. That would be a reasonable political conclusion to draw from a simplified "back to 1914" assessment which foregrounds inter-imperialist conflict without examining the differences in the world system today.

If, on the other hand, the new elements in capitalist globalisation are acknowledged (without, again, being turned into the whole story) then it is more obvious that there is only one power which aspires to dominate and police the unfolding world system, and one world imperial power nexus which aims at the oppression or exploitation of most of the world's peoples, and that is the system centred on the USA. That is the main political difference with the world of a century ago, where there was no power, even the British Empire, which could really hope to dominate the world, and all the leading powers were at analogous levels of economic development. That being the case, building the broadest possible front against today's ambitious global hegemon, including exploiting the real differences between the US and its allies on the one hand and other capitalist powers on the other, becomes sensible politics for anti-imperialists. But if one regards the Russia and China as equally imperialistic (or even worse in particular circumstances) then the way is clear for a politics of general moralising and indiscriminate condemnation of all parties in any clash between those parties outside the US-led system of power and those within it.

So an understanding of the Ukraine crisis and an evaluation of its politics from the international perspective has to start with a more detailed understanding at the actual imperialism of today, rather than a timeless "imperialism" disconnected from contemporary reality.

Imperialism: super-, ultra- or inter-?

In that setting, what is the structure of the 21st century imperialist world order? Since 1991 the most decisive single element in international politics has been the US attempt to secure, by force or otherwise, a hegemony which would permit the continued domination of its own ruling economic interests, presented as operating for the general good of humanity. The world order the US seeks to enforce also, and not incidentally, allows the ruling economic interests of the US itself and its closest allies in the G7 to reap benefits beyond what Kiernan's "simple commercial exchange" would yield. Inequalities of power relations are embedded in the system of commercial exchange, and it is these that the US and its allies seek to reproduce.

Three different abstract political "models" could be consistent with this general order and the prevailing balance of economic power – super-imperialism; inter-imperialist rivalry; and ultra-imperialism. Super-imperialism assumes the world system is dominated by a single imperialist power, which rules all the rest, from lesser imperialist powers down to states which are not really powers at all, even perhaps within their own national borders. Inter-imperialist competition argues for a continuing struggle for markets, influence and control by several powers, or blocs of powers, within a world system that tries to resolve their antagonisms on a bilateral or multilateral basis, but without either an overarching hegemonic regulator or combined authoritative mediating structures. Ultra-imperialism postulates the merging of competing imperialisms into one integrated system, somewhat analogous to monopoly capitalist mergers. It differs from super-imperialism in that there is no one power commanding the others, and assumes a radical diminution of the capacity of the nation-state as a point of organisation and power for capital accumulation. Lenin used the terms 'super-imperialism' and 'ultra-imperialism' interchangeably – understandably so, since the idea of a single imperial power overwhelming all others, rather than all of them fusing together, was inconceivable 100 years ago. Here we make a distinction between the drive for undisputed world hegemony by the US (super-imperialism), and the process of the elaboration of institutions and policies which embody the collective interests of world imperialism (ultra-imperialism), closely entwined as these two concepts evidently are.

In reality, since the emergence of modern capitalist imperialism in the late 19th century, the world system has always been a mixture of all three aspects, and it is so today – never has the world order corresponded entirely to one or the other. Even during the First World War, when inter-imperialist rivalry was dominant enough to send millions of soldiers to the slaughter, the President of the USA stood out for a new coalition of civilised nations to rule the world, and no colonial power pushed its antipathy to its rivals to the point of allowing any subject peoples to escape the domination of imperialism entirely. World War Two concluded in the Asia-Pacific theatre (where that war's imperialist nature was least disguised) with the British military deploying Japanese troops to help restore French rule in Indochina, and using its own to restore Dutch colonial authority in Indonesia! US super-imperialism emerged during World War Two, and extended its scope after 1991, but it has never been entirely unchallenged by capitalist rivals.

Let us look at the different models as they might apply to the world today, and at how they bleed over into each other:

First, this could be a super-imperialist world, in which capitalist accumulation proceeds peaceably (in that the great capitalist states do not fight each other at any rate) under the hegemony of one power. There is only one contender for the hegemon, of course – the USA. However, the relative and increasingly exposed weakness of the USA, its economy barely recovered from the catastrophic slump (it's debt has gone beyond the IMF ' serious risk' level) and possibly surpassed in the gross dimensions of economic power by China; its currency's reserve role, with all the benefits of deficit covering that entails, increasingly at the mercy on the continued willingness of others (Beijing above all) to hold it; and its armed forces fought to a standstill in Iraq and Afghanistan, all point to its waning relative power. On the other hand, it remains the leading world power by several orders of magnitude, and of course its military dwarfs any combination which could conceivably be assembled against it. US bases are everywhere. It is the single loudest voice in the counsels of NATO and the IMF. Putative rivals would rather be its friend. Even Britain pre-1914 could not lay claim to a comparable position of world domination – Royal Navy notwithstanding, it was only first amongst equals.

The extent and importance of that relative decline is disputed. But the ambitious attempt to create a stable super-imperialist system after 1991 is failing, while remaining the single most potent factor in world politics – a combustible dynamic. The failure is rooted not just in that decline in US power vis-à-vis its rivals, leaving Washington simply short on the power and resources requires to dominate the whole world, although this is a point which continues to elude the more chauvinistic and utopian presidential contenders. It is also because super-imperialism requires the hegemon to construct an order which takes full account of the interests of lesser powers, in order that their elites can continue to feel their own position remains best secured by acquiescence in the world economic/political architecture capped by a beneficent super-imperialism. The experience of the Bush-Cheney administration, quite apart from any underlying exacerbation of US weaknesses, established that the US could not fulfil this role – it could neither exercise the coercive force nor maintain the consensus necessary to accommodate the interests of all powers, particularly Russia and China. The Obama administration is still giving this project a go, with more emollient tactics but without any spectacular success, and his successor, of whichever party, will most likely revert to still more aggressive tactics. The US-led world system, often masquerading as the "international community" in toto, continues to incorporate the ruling groups in Britain, France, Germany, Japan, Australia, Canada, Italy and other smaller states. But hegemony over China and

Russia, at the very least, is not on the agenda – the moment when it might have been, after 1991, is now behind us. A world order pivoting on the unchallenged supremacy of US power is therefore beyond reach. The greatest danger of war in general arises from the fact that Washington cannot and will not accommodate to this fact without a struggle. Certainly, a system dependent on the use (or threat of it) of US military power will not provide a stable basis for international relations. Bush and Cheney tested that perspective to the point of destruction and beyond.

Some hold out the prospect of a different great power rising before long, one based around a new cycle of capital accumulation based in the Far East, centred of course on China, and this power assuming globally hegemonic dimensions. At the measured theoretical level that is the argument of the late Giovanni Arrighi in his Adam Smith in Beijing, his last work, although it was his view that such an order need not necessarily be "imperialist". It also lies behind the profusion of "China to Rule the World" literature emitted in recent times, and the more so because of Beijing's apparent skill in escaping the worst consequences of the global crash to date. Of course, it is one thing to acknowledge that China is ascending in wealth and power, quite another to extrapolate this fifty years forward, assuming no intervening crisis or counter-movement, and declare an imminent Chinese world.

At present an East Asian-based system of global hegemony does not exist, and it could only come into being, even hypothetically, through a clash of some kind between China and the USA, unless we are to posit a future in which Washington does what no hegemon has previously done and yield its positions without a fight. This is a fight which the US, with its vast and growing military assets across the Pacific/East Asia region, seems to be preparing for. The escalating tensions in the region between several different powers indicate that any hypothetical super-imperialism in the east would lack even the foundations which the US presently enjoys, and would in any case have to proceed through the furnace of great power conflict – it is in this part of the world that the logic which led to 1914 seems to cast the longest shadow.

So it would seem that any attempt to either maintain the vanishing super-imperialism or replace it with a new one must in fact lead in the direction of the second "model" of world political organisation for capital accumulation– inter-imperialist struggle. Under this scenario, the existing tendencies towards the formation of competing blocs and the emergence of new "great powers" come to predominate and eventually leads to clashes, between the US-led bloc of powers (not itself monolithic, of course) and Russia or China or both. There was no lack of evidence for such a scenario even before the Ukraine crisis – the overt challenge to US power from Russia in parts of the former USSR, starting with the war with Georgia in 2008 (a challenge which also divided to some extent the US from its European allies); the inability of Washington to forge a consensus behind its aggression in Iraq in 2003 (in contrast to 1991) and the present divisions over Syria and Iran in the Middle East accompanying a fragmentation of the traditional US power alliances across the region; and the multiplying signs of friction in relations between China and the USA and its principal Asian allies, Japan and South Korea. "Multipolarity" is back, with all that such rivalry has historically entailed.

While such a perspective inevitably conjures up the ghosts of 1914 and 1939, this road too is relatively blocked at present. The mechanisms of globalisation work against an acute sharpening of capitalist rivalries, by expanding the cosmopolitan nature of capital accumulation, across and regardless of most state boundaries driven by global banks and transnational corporations. Moreover, at the state level, US military power can be challenged locally and specifically (as the Iraqi resistance and the Taliban have established), but not in any form of major conventional confrontation. Here the 1914 analogy does not hold, at least for the present. That does not prevent the unfolding of a system of dynamic rivalry, but it circumscribes it. Today the USA is not powerful enough to maintain its place on the super-imperial throne, but is too powerful to be pushed off it either.

A circumscribed, 21st century, inter-imperialist model would therefore postulate trade wars, proxy wars, the development of blocs with the expansion of some capitalist nation-states into "vacant" (non-bloc) territory at the expense of others, conflicts over resources (a struggle fought by coups etc in resource-holding countries) and the incremental breakdown of such international structures for the mediation of conflict as exist, leading towards "small scale" wars where interests collide territorially. That is pretty much the world as it is, and the world into which the Ukraine crisis fits as a leading symptom. However, the circumscribed nature of the rivalry (limited at least for the foreseeable future absent the much more rapid rise of a Chinese power which takes a more aggressive turn) also pushes the regime of accumulation in the direction of the third abstract model – ultra-imperialism, in which international structures serving the interests of imperialism in general, and underpinned by the internationalisation of finance capital and monopoly, ensure the security and development of the world system.

Lenin had something to say about this concept in 1916. He observed that "there is no doubt that the development is going in the direction of a single world trust that will swallow up all enterprises and states without exception". Ever since, however, only his subsequent qualification that "…the development in this direction is proceeding under such stress, with such a tempo, with such contradiction, conflicts and convulsions….that before a single world trust will be reached, before the respective national finance capitals will have formed a world union of 'ultra-imperialism', imperialism will inevitably explode, capitalism will turn into its opposite" has generally been recalled. [10]

Lenin's qualification seems unexceptionable given the time and circumstances he was writing in. Indeed, imperialism was "exploding" all around him. However, nearly one hundred years on, we should equally attend to the original proposition that the logic of capital accumulation does indeed tend in the direction of ultra-imperialism. Lenin would be surprised to find imperialism still with us in 2015 but, given its continued existence, he might not be so shocked to learn that the forms of ultra-imperialism had indeed proliferated. These forms – NATO, European Union, IMF, World Bank, World Trade Organisation, G7/8 – were for the most part originally forged to consolidate bourgeois solidarity in the confrontation with Communism. They now hold a renewed lease on life as instruments of the collective hegemony of the great centres of capitalism over the rest of the world, organising the globe for their mutual benefit and charged in particular with removing all impediments standing in the way of realising the ideal of a frictionless global process of capital accumulation.

While ultra-imperialism, an idea which traces its lineage back to Karl Kautsky, has not come to pass in any complete form the tendencies leading in its direction have grown stronger, and have a direct bearing on world politics today. Could this momentum, initially expressed as the collective interest of the existing power-centres of capitalism against the rest of the world, prevail over the counter-trends identified above?

For some, most notably the theorists Antonio Negri and Michael Hardt, it already has.

Their book Empire, became a best-seller around the turn of the century despite, or perhaps because, it obscured the real developments in contemporary imperialism, dissolving the latter in a world "empire" without imperialists or states confronting a "multitude" without classes, parties or perspectives. Its theme has been picked up by others since, including those who have developed the theory of a "global imperialism" detached not just from particular states, but from any reliance on extra-economic coercive power. [11]

The illusions advanced by Hardt and Negri – beyond the purely comic ideas that the corporations are striving to make the workplace "fun" and that the new political model of struggle should be based upon St Francis of Assisi - include that the United Nations and international law now reign supreme, that corporations no longer have any state-based home, that imperialism has no territorial imperative and that the act of migration is the most revolutionary decision the individual could make today. Essentially, they take contemporary capitalism at its own valuation as a global friction-free entity in which states have surrendered pride of place to corporations and struggles located anywhere (as opposed to everywhere) are now redundant.

This breaks with the understanding, common to Lenin, Luxemburg and more recent anti-imperialist theorists that "the manifestations of imperialism are to be explained by the lack of homogeneity of the capitalist world economy", in the words of the late Marxist economist Ernest Mandel. Were it otherwise, there would be a global equalisation of the rate of profit, no scope for super-profit, secured by coercion or otherwise, and hence no basis for inter-imperialist rivalry on a capitalist basis, and ultimately therefore no basis for imperialist war. Any war, in such an unfeasible situation, would be waged by a monolithic elite driven by the requirements of accumulation through ever-intensifying exploitation, against the world's population. [12] Taken altogether, the Hardt/Negri line of argument absolved the USA of any responsibility for the state of the world or its actions therein – indeed, they argued that it was simply acting as a guardian of the world order at the request of the world itself, in the same way as Augustus took the imperial mantle in Rome at the behest of the Senate. Developing this line of argument, they assert that "all interventions of the imperial armies are solicited by one or more of the parties involved in an already existing conflict", just one of many Hardt/Negri formulations utterly refuted by the Iraq war.

As the Argentinean academic and campaigner Atilio Boron observed in his powerful refutation of the Hardt/Negri thesis: "the favourable reception given by the establishment's mandarins to Empire show that they read the book carefully, that they correctly understood its most profound message, and that they accurately concluded that there was nothing within the book that could be considered incompatible with the dominant ideology or with the self-image that the powerful like to exhibit." [13]

Boron deals with some of their briefly-fashionable fantasising in summary form. If you doubt the nature of the relationship of trans-national corporations to nation-based states, just try nationalising their local assets and see who comes protesting – almost certainly the Ambassador of one state or another, he points out. Indeed, to take just one contemporary example amongst many, when Russia moved against Shell and BP in 2007, it was Tony Blair himself who led the lobbying on behalf of these British-centred companies. While the Dow Chemical executive who talked wistfully of buying an island as "truly neutral ground" to headquarter his company so it could become genuinely non-national no doubt expressed a deep desire among business leaders for a world they could bestride unencumbered by considerations of parochial identity or taxation, there is little doubt that it is the US State Department which Dow would call from its island should its assets be threatened by any state actor. [14]

Hardt's criticisms of the anti-war movement of 2002-03 for failing to march in line with his perspectives were perhaps sufficient admission of this. Just days after the largest global demonstrations in human history – February 15 2003 – against the incipient aggression by the real Empire of the USA against the real territory of Iraq without the slightest sign of UN approval – he admonished the marchers for missing the point – indeed, falling into the "trap" of supporting those against the war and opposing those promoting it! Railing against the anti-Americanism which only he and Bush-Blair had detected in the demonstrations, Hardt regretted that such energy was not being channelled into "global network connections with a global vision of possible futures." The idea that February 15 was the result of the global network of the anti-war movements united around a determination to assert a future based on life against imperialism appears to have passed the professor by. [15]

Negri subsequently asserted that the US role in Iraq was "nation-building" and "democratising", thereby affecting a complete synthesis of the opinions of the radical Italian academic and the then-President of the United States. Bizarrely, he saw the United Nations' endorsement of the US occupation of Iraq in 2003 as a sign of the Bush administration bowing the knee to the world body, when almost the entirety of global opinion could see that the reverse was true. As Ellen Meiksins Wood mildly observed "such views not only miss something truly essential in today's global order but also leave us powerless to resist the empire of capital." [16]

Hardt/Negri presented an idealised, utopian, view of an ultra-imperialist world. Not only does it scarcely correspond to today's reality, there is no easy path which might lead us to such a place either. Nevertheless, globalisation allied to a range of global bodies, often transforming them somewhat in the process, has created instruments which make a developed ultra-imperialism not merely a fantasy. Worldwide management of capital accumulation, and enforcement of its requirements in controlling the terms of investment, trade, labour supply and political interventions, is a serious prospect, albeit not a benign one. The actual institutions which provide the scaffolding of ultra-imperialism are instruments of combat in the hands of the great powers, or fields of struggle between them. The United Nations, which might appear to be the most obvious exception – indeed, it might stand outside the apparatus of ultra-imperialism altogether – has been radically degraded in the post-1991 era, quite contrary to the rosy liberal prognostications of the time. It was simply ignored when the US wanted to launch war against Yugoslavia, and brushed aside in a far more overt and humiliating fashion by Bush and Blair when they attacked Iraq in 2003. It has never truly recovered.

Those organisations which do play a vital function on a world scale, like NATO, the International Monetary Fund or the World Trade Organisation do so primarily as projections of US power, although the interests of others are obviously to some extent accommodated. US domination has been made abundantly plain, if anyone doubted it, by the behaviour of both bodies during the Ukrainian and Greek crises in 2014-15. To the extent that other states – Germany of France for example – have promoted different views as to how these institutions should conduct themselves their push-back has not generated sufficient friction to transform them from sites of inter-imperial difference to a full-blown ultra-imperialism.

Nevertheless, it is fair to question the degree to which these conflicts and rivalries can be presented as extending as far as a full struggle for the redivision of the world, in the sense that Lenin described it. This has a critical bearing on the Ukraine conflict. World markets are more integrated than ever before, even if priority access to super-profitable key resources is often determined by mixture of violence and corruption rather than competitive economic mechanisms. However, exclusive control of markets and resources in the interests of one particular big power is a rarity. Coercion abroad is certainly exerted by great powers to secure better profits for monopoly capital, but this seldom has the zero-sum consequences for other powers that it might have done in the high days of classical imperialism (although even then foreign firms were seldom entirely excluded from the colonial empires of particular powers). Furthermore, the USA has declared almost every part of the globe a zone of "special interest" to itself, as we shall see. This circumscribes the capacity of other powers to establish their own exclusive areas of control. They rely instead on the US "cutting them in" as a rewards for good behaviour – cooperation in its imperial ventures. This may work well enough for British or French oil companies in the Middle East, for example; but powers which stand outside the US world order architecture – even to a limited degree – like Russia and China get no such latitude. Here great power rivalry corresponds more closely to the old models. This unity of struggle and rivalry between and among the centres of world capitalism has been played out over Ukraine.

The Hardt/Negri ultra-imperialist "Empire" contradicted the movement of life itself. That empire – the real one starting wars around the world – bears many of the hallmarks of an ultra-imperialism. But it does so under the acknowledged leadership of one state, the USA. And that state made its own plans.

The Pentagon's Unipolar Planning

The nation-state muscle refuting the Hardt/Negri analysis came from the Pentagon, unsurprisingly. Hardly had the hammer-and-sickle been lowered from over the Kremlin for the last time as 1991 became 1992 than what would become the core of the US neo-conservative political lobby were ready with their plan.

The Department of Defence Planning Guidance for 1994-1999 was prepared early in 1992 and was the work of Paul Wolfowitz, Lewis Libby and Zalmay Khalilzad, three figures who were in due course to play a leading part in the foreign policy adventures of the younger Bush's presidency. The Defence Secretary of the time was Dick Cheney, the main architect of the Iraq War and more besides, a conservative imperialist to his cowboy boots. Innocent of Marxist categories as they likely were – although as Richard Sakwa has observed, "the Trotskyist roots of neocon thinking are well known, and for them world revolution was...only transformed: the fight now was not for revolutionary socialism but for capitalist democracy" – they would not have understood they were preparing a charter for super-imperialism. But they were. [17]

Given the influence the document has had on world politics since, and the particular ways in which it has informed the US approach to the Ukraine crisis, it is worth extensive quotation, as originally leaked to the *New York Times*:

"Our first objective is to prevent the re-emergence of a new rival, either on the territory of the former Soviet Union or elsewhere, that poses a threat on the order of that posed formerly by the Soviet Union. This is a dominant consideration underlying the new regional defense strategy and requires that we endeavor to prevent any hostile power from dominating a region whose resources would, under consolidated control, be sufficient to generate global power. These regions include Western Europe, East Asia, the territory of the former Soviet Union, and Southwest Asia.

"There are three additional aspects to this objective: First, the U.S. must show the leadership necessary to establish and protect a new order that holds the promise of convincing potential competitors that they need not aspire to a greater role or pursue a more aggressive posture to protect their legitimate interests. Second, in the non-defense areas, we must account sufficiently for the interests of the advanced industrial nations to discourage them from challenging our leadership or seeking to overturn the established political and economic order. Finally, we must maintain the mechanisms for deterring potential competitors from even aspiring to a larger regional or global role. An effective reconstitution capability is important here, since it implies that a potential rival could not hope to quickly or easily gain a predominant military position in the world.

"The second objective is to address sources of regional conflict and instability in such a way as to promote increasing respect for international law, limit international violence, and encourage the spread of democratic forms of government and open economic systems. These objectives are especially important in deterring conflicts or threats in regions of security importance to the United States because of their proximity (such as Latin America), or where we have treaty obligations or security commitments to other nations. While the U.S. cannot become the world's "policeman" by assuming responsibility for righting every wrong, we will retain the pre-eminent responsibility for addressing selectively those wrongs which threaten not only our interests, but those of our allies or friends, or which could seriously unsettle international relations. Various types of U.S. interests may be involved in such instances: access to vital raw materials, primarily Persian Gulf oil; proliferation of weapons of mass destruction and ballistic missiles, threats to U.S. citizens from terrorism or regional or local conflict, and threats to U.S. society from narcotics trafficking. . . ."

"There are other potential nations or coalitions that could, in the further future, develop strategic aims and a defense posture of region-wide or global domination. Our strategy must now refocus on precluding the emergence of any potential future global competitor. But because we no longer face either a global threat or a hostile, non-democratic power dominating a region critical to our interests, we have the opportunity to meet threats at lower levels and lower costs -- as long as we are prepared to reconstitute additional forces should the need to counter a global threat re-emerge...

"NATO continues to provide the indispensable foundation for a stable security environment in Europe. Therefore, it is of fundamental importance to preserve NATO as the primary instrument of Western defense and security, as well as the channel for U.S. influence and participation in European security affairs. While the United States supports the goal of European integration, we must seek to prevent the emergence of

European-only security arrangements which would undermine NATO, particularly the alliance's integrated command structure. . . .

"The end of the Warsaw Pact and the dissolution of the Soviet Union have gone a long way toward increasing stability and reducing the military threat to Europe. The ascendancy of democratic reformers in the Russian republic, should this process continue, is likely to create a more benign policy toward Eastern Europe. However, the U.S. must keep in mind the long history of conflict between the states of Eastern Europe, as well as the potential for conflict between the states of Eastern Europe and those of the former Soviet Union. . . ." [18]

This is the most clearly-expressed charter for US unilateral world domination, or a form of super-imperialism. While drafted for a Republican administration, all its assumptions and many of its strategic choices have informed the policies of all US Presidents since. Its spirit is still abroad in US politics. To take one example, Florida Senator Marco Rubio, at time of writing one of the leading candidates for the 2016 Republican presidential nomination has spelt out a military policy which in some respects goes perhaps even further. "As President, I will use American power to oppose any violations of international waters, airspace, cyberspace or outer space," he has said. "This includes the economic disruptions caused when one country invades another, as well as the chaos caused by disruptions in choke points such as the South China Sea or the Strait of Hormuz." In its reach Plan Rubio goes beyond even concepts of super-imperialism or "world policeman" to intergalactic enforcer; with the US deploying its armed force to unilaterally organise affairs to its liking across the entirety of the globe's surface and beyond. Rubio is not an anachronism in US politics either. [19]

The Pentagon plan was a nuanced document, in some respects. While setting its sight on a US-dominated world, it also acknowledged that super-imperialism would have to depend in part on the creation of multilateral institutions which could reflect other interests – ultra-imperialism. In particular, its recognition that a stable and lasting US world hegemony would need to accommodate the interests of at least some other powers imposed requirements which official Washington has struggled to meet, at least consistently. The failure to even gesture towards understanding and accommodating specific Russian interests has obviously had a bearing on the Ukrainian crisis. Russia, like China, now stands outside the US-dominated system. It has tried to join the club, and its elite is still hopeful of eventual admission. But successive US administrations have taken the view that the Russians simply need to be taught to "eat their spinach" in the words of neo-conservative Victoria Nuland, who later emerged to play the part of neo-colonial overlord towards Ukraine in 2013-14. There have been warning signs – Russia declined to take part in the aggression against Yugoslavia despite pressure, and was indeed mildly unhelpful to the NATO operation, despite then-President Yeltsin's unequivocal pro-western orientation. The Georgian war of 2008, which gave a US-aligned government in Tiblisi a bloody nose when it sought to attack the breakaway province of South Ossetia, was another clear warning that the US needed to take better account of Russia's immediate interests. [19]

But while a unipolar system is consistent with some large planets in orbit around it, it cannot easily coexist with another source of gravitational pull, however weak, it seems.

New NATO

As the Wolfowitz doctrine foreshadowed, the role of NATO was to be crucial in the new order, notwithstanding that the ostensible reason for its foundation and maintenance for more than forty years no longer existed. NATO was created in 1949, uniting the USA and Canada with much of Western Europe in a military alliance supposed to deter Soviet aggression in the continent. Similar blocs were established in the Middle East and in South-East Asia.

Neither at the time nor since has there been any evidence that such an aggression was even contemplated by the USSR. Instead, NATO became a bloc designed as much to keep its own members in line – recall the threats as to what would happen to Italy should its citizens have been so unwise as to elect a Communist government in the 1970s – as to deter anyone else.

Nevertheless, the end of the Cold War provided a good opportunity to review NATO's purpose and, declaring mission accomplished, wind it up (the Soviet-led Warsaw Treaty Organisation, founded in 1955, was indeed dissolved). This is not what happened of course. Despite promises, or at the very least understandings, offered to the Soviet government in 1990 and 1991 when German reunification was on the agenda NATO instead embarked on a programme of headlong expansion along two axis. First, it took in new members throughout Eastern Europe and even among ex-Soviet republics themselves, in effect pushing the military alliance right up against Russia's new borders. Second, it began to undertake actual military operations well outside its previous zone of operation and, indeed, outside any geographically-based notion as to what might constitute the "north Atlantic".

These two developments illustrated the changed role for NATO envisaged in the new unipolar world of a single super-imperial power ruling in the name of itself and of all simultaneously.

The first actual outing in earnest for the "new NATO" was the war of intervention in the territory of the former Yugoslavia, culminating in the Kosovo conflict in 1999. In the latter war, NATO acted without any international legal sanction, declaring that it was bombing Yugoslav infrastructure and forces as executor of the will of a self-defined "international community" – a community which excluded, amongst many others, China, Russia and India, all of whom opposed NATO's actions while in practice acquiescing in them. Among the long-lasting diplomatic consequences of the Yugoslav war was the degradation of the United Nations, which had been ascribed a new pivotal role by liberal and social-democratic circles in the post-1991 world. It was envisaged as assuming the world regulation mandate which it should have had in 1945 but had been stymied ever after by the bipolar world which emerged, Security Council vetoes and all. In 1999, the UN was simply ignored (since Russia for sure would have vetoed the Kosovan war), and it became evident that the USA, using NATO, could and would go to war without asking anyone else's permission.

NATO's next war was even further from the north Atlantic. The organisation invoked its "self-defence" clause after the 9/11 attacks on New York City and Washington, and piled in behind the Bush administration as it launched its war on Afghanistan, leading to a military occupation which persists to this day. On this occasion, some form of United Nations authority was given for the initial US measures to attack those held responsible for 9/11, but not for the prolonged military occupation which ensued. The Afghan war (the fourth of the imperialist epoch) underlined NATO's changed mission – to act as the military arm of the US power in ordering the world, if and when Washington preferred to not act, or be seen to act, unilaterally.

From there it was only a fairly small step to the overt aggression against Iraq. Here, securing United Nations sanction for the war was trifled with by Bush and British Prime Minister Tony Blair, but then dismissed as irrelevant when it became clear that such authority would not be forthcoming. Nor was the Iraq war a NATO operation, since two of the most significant European powers in NATO – France and Germany – remained opposed to the invasion. The US did however secure backing – mainly rhetorical – from the newer East European NATO member states. Pentagon chief Donald Rumsfeld famously contrasted the compliance of "new Europe" as against the recalcitrance of "old Europe" in bending to Washington's purposes.

The Iraq war ended up undermining the unipolar world, militarily and politically. The incapacity of the USA to follow-up the overthrow of Saddam Hussein and the dissolution of his Baath regime by pacifying a country in the grip of a rapidly-widening insurrection against the occupation exposed the limitations of the over-weening military resources of the USA. And the divisions engendered by the wilful decision to ignore international law reverberate to this day. The Iraq War did underline, however, that the US was perfectly willing to act as the unilateral "super-imperial power", without any endorsement from the residually "ultra-imperial" NATO if needs be.

NATO's final military outing to date was the aerial attack on Libya in 2011. This was given a patina of United Nations benediction, in that the international body endorsed action to prevent the supposedly impending massacre which the Gaddafi regime was going to visit on the people of Benghazi. In fact, and as warned by many at the time, the NATO air action rapidly developed into a further (and illegitimate) regime change war, in effect tilting an otherwise unfavourable military balance in favour of the anti-Gaddafi forces in the civil conflict. Gaddafi's embrace of Tony Blair and support for the new dispensation in the world after 2003 availed him naught. This war was pressed for most actively by the French and British governments (in the case of the former in explicit, if secret at the time, guarantees of preferential treatment for French oil and other business interests, philosophically negotiated by Bernard Henri-Levy) and it had the endorsement of the assorted autocrats and despots of the Arab League. However, even the limited air operation undertaken by Britain and France would not have been possible without US practical support, despite US Vice-President Joe Biden making it clear that Washington had little interest in what happened in Libya. Here NATO fulfilled both a contemporary neo-colonial role, and a classical ultra-imperialist one, mobilising a range of great powers behind a political project initiated by just two of them – and all this with philosophical sanction! [19]

The record of conflicts fought therefore indicates the range of roles NATO can play, but always at the ultimate discretion and direction of the US government. It should also be noted that the wars in Yugoslavia, Iraq and Libya (once it moved to the regime change stage) were all fought in the face of Russian opposition. Only the attack on Afghanistan had the support of Moscow. Clearly, if the new NATO was not explicitly directed against Russia, as the original model had been, nor was it in the slightest degree willing to accommodate the latter's views and interests, even on matters close to its borders.

As important has been NATO's relentless eastward expansion since 1991. The USSR's German ally, the German Democratic Republic, was absorbed into NATO with German reunification. But the real march eastwards began in 1999, when Poland, Hungary and the Czech Republic joined, over vociferous opposition from the normally tractable Boris Yeltsin, then still Russian President. Brushing aside these continuing objections and warnings from the Kremlin, seven further countries were incorporated into NATO in 2004. These included three former Soviet allies – Bulgaria, Romania and Slovakia, and three states which had been part of the USSR itself – the Baltic republics of Latvia, Estonia and Lithuania. In the course of this century three other socialist countries not allied to the USSR – former Yugoslav republics Croatia and Slovenia, and Albania, have also joined NATO. The only concession to Russian opinion was that, initially, western military forces were not deployed to the territory of the new entrants. [20]

Ostensibly, these states were seeking US military protection against any danger of a recrudescent Russian threat, regardless of the absence of any evidence of such a threat. In reality – and not discounting popular worries about Russian intentions, rooted in history – they see NATO membership as an entry-point to the "new world order" as privileged allies of US hyperpower. The price to be paid was support for the Bush-Blair aggression against Iraq; their reward was Rumsfeld's "new Europe" pat on the head. These countries also offered themselves up as bases for Washington's forward missile-defence schemes – the "star wars" plans of old – directed against Russia. Regardless of internal differences, the elites of eastern Europe mostly want in to the US embrace. Today, NATO is establishing command centres in the three Baltic republics and Poland, Romania and Bulgaria, as well as beefing up its rapid reaction forces. These are of course mainly directed against Russia, but also give NATO an enhanced capacity to intervene in the Middle East or North Africa at a moment's notice. [21]

From this brief survey of NATO's post-1991 history, a few conclusion can be drawn about the organisation's present nature. It is above all an instrument of US super-imperialism – it undertakes no operations which Washington does not support politically, and cannot function without US military underpinning. In implementing Washington's will, it is no longer bounded by either geographical or mission-based constraints – anywhere, anytime, for any purpose, not just the "self-defence" of its founding charter. At the same time, NATO has enough scope to implement the projects of other major powers in its ranks – the Anglo-French bombing of Libya, for example – as long as the US can be persuaded to go along. To that extent, it has an ultra-imperialist aspect, in the more nuanced terms of the 1992 Pentagon plan. NATO is not, however, indispensable to the US – if its members cannot be cajoled into endorsing a US-led war, as in Iraq, the US simply proceeds regardless with such national allies as want to sign up. The idea of NATO actually opposing a US military initiative is entirely fanciful. NATO is used as a military and diplomatic lever to draw states into the general orbit of US power. And it never pays any attention to the views of Moscow. This is the NATO which Washington wants to extend into Ukraine, right up to the border – until a generation ago, not a border at all – of Russia, in Donbas, Kharkiv and elsewhere. Even, in the Pentagon's dreams, the great naval port of Sevastopol was within reach, with the US navy berthing where once the Red Army had defied the Nazi invaders.

NATO's closest helper in the imposition of the priorities of super-imperialism is the International Monetary Fund. Its mission has been to enforce the "Washington consensus" on the indebted nations of the world – the reduction of social expenditure, the privatisation of state assets, the removal of regulations and the curbing of the rights of labour. It complements the threat of military coercion embodied in NATO with the imposition of economic coercion to force the compliance of sovereign states with the priorities of global capital. Its general role in this respect is well-known, and the crisis in Greece has made it more so. Less advertised is the care it takes to ensure that its activities do not diminish imperialism's fighting capacities. However indebted or impoverished a country that comes to the IMF for relief may be, the institution never, under any circumstances, recommends a cut in defence spending. And replace with The decisive voice and vote in the IMF's proceedings is without doubt Washington's.

European Union – Partner and Rival

The European Union is perhaps the other great institution both of the "unipolar" ultra-imperial world and of second order (for the present) multi-polar rivalry. Its post-1991 development indicates the dynamics underpinning and at the same time undermining the world system the US has put in place.

A *Financial Times* columnist, John Kay, outlined at the height of the Greek crisis how he had become convinced that the EU:

> "was an imperialist project. Those who proclaimed the British empire used to sing: 'wider still and wider may thy bounds be set/God who made thee mighty, make thee mightier yet'....the expansion of the EU embraced a similar vision...
>
> "The boundaries of western Europe have been pushed as far east as at any time in history, save for the best forgotten precedent of the Nazi occupation of most of the continent in 1941-42. The Ukraine crisis tests how far implied promises of political, economic and ultimately military support in that extension will be maintained when called on."

Kay ended by invoking the familiar themes of imperial over-stretch. However, like all previous empires, the EU will likely only become aware that it has stretched too far when it is too late to wind back in peacefully. [22]

The genesis of the EU is well-known. Originally an industrial bloc uniting German and French capital in the coal and steel industries (the first efforts to establish which were the creation of an iron and steel cartel between the two big powers plus Belgium and Luxembourg as long ago as 1927), it expanded by degrees to become first a free-trade area, then a deeper "single market" and finally an integrated economic space governed by its own institutions and embracing nearly all of western Europe as socialism dissolved in the eastern half of the continent. By the turn of the century, the EU was assuming some of the attributes of a federal state, although not all that many. It had introduced a common currency – a landmark step towards a form of federalism – which covered most, but not all, of its member states, but it had taken only the most hesitant and half-formed steps towards a common military and foreign policy, normally the preserves of the federal level in such constitutional arrangements. Rhetoric aside, such power resided at the nation-state level – mainly the British, French and the German. [23] It had also opened its doors to the former socialist states of Eastern Europe, in the same way and to more-or-less the same extent as NATO. In doing so, it had set aside its own standards for political reasons to some extent, embracing Romania and Bulgaria despite their entrenched judicial and police corruption and inadequate democratic governance. The result, to date, has been the creation of an economic behemoth with a capitalist market larger than the US, but in which the decisive locus of political authority remained, not with its constituent nation states in all cases, nor with its federal institutions either, but with the largest amongst them – Germany above all, and France secondarily.

The EU is a hybrid imperial structure internally and is integrated into the US world order as both partner and sometime rival, externally. It has proved an effective institution for consolidating and extending capitalism across Europe. In doing so it has worked mainly in the interests of the big corporations of the largest member states, Germany and France. At one level that says no more than observing that most of the biggest companies in the USA are headquartered in the New York area or in California. All are subject to the same rules and framework, set at the "federal" level in Brussels. However, the Greek crisis has made it abundantly clear that the German government calls the shots, with the EU Commission functioning as little more than the executor of Berlin's policy, as perhaps slightly modified by Paris. And there is little doubt that the EU has both expressed and expedited the abatement of the rivalry between French and German capitalisms, which had contributed to three major wars in seventy years between the two. Here German imperialism follows similar objectives to those it did in the twentieth century, albeit with far more agreeable methods.

The US government long supported the development of the EU, as part of a strong common front of the major capitalist powers against communism. Only after 1991 did the possibility start to emerge that it could be a serious rival on the global stage. These fears, which Washington sought to mitigate as far as it could by promoting the Union's eastwards extension – even for a time including Turkey - as a means of diluting its political coherence, were always a bit overdrawn. After all, as noted, military, diplomatic and the greater part of political power was still devolved to the member states. In that context the growing euro-scepticism in British politics (Britain having joined the EU late, in 1973) was useful – it inhibited the federal pretensions of Germany and its "satellite politicians" in other states. The EU as an economic giant left official Washington relatively untroubled (Japan was long the big fear in the US in that respect), as long as it remained politically weak. This has been official London's perspective for the last generation too. This British view is not only the customary genuflexion to the "special relationship". It also coincides with the interests of British finance capital, expressed through the City of London, which does not see its ambitions as circumscribed by the European continent, and acts as a finance centre for all parts of the globe. It finds European free trade desirable (as a component of global free trade), but baulks at any tendency in the EU which might shut London off from, or reduce access to, money and markets elsewhere in the world.

But the EU has changed as it has grown, and in ways that bear on the Ukraine crisis directly. For one thing, while older member states have been able to retain independent or neutral military alignments (Ireland, Finland, Austria inter alia), new entrants are now required to adopt a common security policy identified with NATO's, which is to say with those EU member-states which are closely allied to the USA. Brussels has also long been agitating to create at least the outline structure of the EU's own military power, drawing on the resources of member states but placing them under an integrated command, and oriented towards rapid deployment in neo-colonial conflicts. And in the last few years, the EU has established its own diplomatic service, controlled by a new Presidency and common representative for foreign affairs. The first holder of the latter office was Catherine Ashton, an apparently soft-headed British social democrat who briefly had a walk-on part in the Ukraine drama. This has certainly strengthened the appearance of federalism in the EU.

At the same time, defence and diplomacy are not core to the EU's mission, at least not yet. The historic offer of the EU to both its founder-members and to the new entrants from the east was instead – democracy and prosperity. The post-2008 crisis has at the very least taken the shine of such claims. The EU institutions, at the instigation of Germany and some of its smaller allies (Finland, Netherlands), have become the unabashed advocates of a capitalist austerity that has impoverished millions of Europeans in the interests of the big German, French and Dutch banks. And those same institutions, building no doubt on their own extremely limited accountability, have become the instruments of an attack on democracy and people's rights. In both Italy and Greece, EU prompting led in 2012 to the replacement of elected governments by technocratic administrations, headed in both cases by alumni of Goldman Sachs, as it happens. Throughout, the EU has insisted that its neo-liberal economic precepts must be followed by all states (at least those within the Eurozone of the single currency) whether the peoples of those states like it, and vote for it, or not. Jose-Manuel Barroso, EU Commission head throughout the crisis (a former Maoist who as the right-wing Prime Minister of Portugal in 2003 led that country into the Iraq War – a war criminal, in effect) has indeed made so bold as to publicly declare that the EU was needed to counterbalance the errors of elected governments. All this has come as a bit of a blow to the broad sections of the left who, with the defeat of the national labour movements in the 1980s (and nowhere more so than in Britain) and the collapse of the USSR, hoped that the ministrations of the European Union with its fabled "social dimension" might offer an alternative route to progress, the EU's overpowering democratic deficit notwithstanding. The Greek crisis of 2015, which featured the institutions of the EU, working mainly to German instructions, bully and bludgeon the elected government of Greece with ever-worse terms for staying in the Euro, callously dooming millions of Greek people to unemployment and poverty, was surely sufficient indicator of the real mission of the EU – serving the needs of finance capital, and in particular the power of its big banks, at all costs.

The further illusion – that the EU at least offered the prospect of peace on a continent that was host to two cataclysmic wars in the first half of the twentieth century by mitigating the inter-imperialist conflicts that had led to these calamities, has been harder-dying. Yet its role in the Ukraine crisis revealed an organisation increasingly driven as much by strategic and geo-political concerns as by simple economic and trade issues. The sensible suggestion that the EU, Ukraine and Russia sit down together to reach a common agreement on trade; and that Russia, by far Ukraine's largest trading partner might have an interest in an association formed between Ukraine and the EU, were dismissed contemptuously by Barroso. In doing so he lifted the edge of the curtain concealing the essence of today's EU as a mainstay of the Washington-dominated imperialist structure, a rival sometimes to be sure, but an ally when the matter is confronting the rising powers outside that structure. While Russia has not viewed the eastward expansion of the EU with quite the same dismay as the extension of NATO, the difference in perspective is narrowing, and with reason. The future of an unchanged EU will be a future of war. [23]

The economic crisis and crumbling unipolarity

Bloodied in Iraq, humiliated in Afghanistan, challenged by China, slapped about the face in Georgia and disrespected by Latin America, the unipolar world order nevertheless staggered on regardless through the first part of this century, like Rasputin taking one bullet after another on top of the poison yet still not succumbing. It took the great banking crash of 2008 to finally put Washington's world in the emergency ward. The economic crisis which has unfolded since, including as it does the partial weakening and discrediting of Washington's claim to world leadership, has further contributed to the conflict in eastern Europe.

This assessment of the political effects of the slump can be taken from three of the best-known spoon-feeders of middle-brow political mush to the transatlantic middle classes. First, Fareed Zakaria then of *Newsweek* and later of *Time*: "The real fallout of the financial crisis will be the delegitmisation of American power. People around the world once saw the United States as the most modern, sophisticated and productive economy in the world. Now they wonder was all this a house of cards? They listened to American policymakers with respect, even awe. Today they wonder if these officials know what they are doing. This loss of credibility will have hard consequences." [24]

And then Philip Stephens of the *Financial Times*, who waxed even more apocalyptic: "The erosion of the west's moral authority that began with the Iraq war has been greatly accelerated…For more than two centuries, the US and Europe have exercised an effortless economic, political and cultural hegemony. That era is ending." Whether "effortless" is the word to describe a system of plunder enforced by war is another matter, of course. [25]

Finally, Gideon Rachman, another *Financial Times* pundit, wrote that the two big obstacles facing the global system as of 2012 were the "sharp fall in America's relative power" and the "loss of faith in the ability of markets to provide order and prosperity to the world system." [26]

All this, it is fair to say, came as a great and most unwelcome shock to the pundits who had been wallowing in the unipolar and uni-ideology moment in world affairs. Clearly, they had been listening too much to Gordon "no more boom and bust" Brown. Had the post-2008 fashion for rediscovering Marx kicked in a few years earlier, perhaps some of the astonished oracles of neo-liberalism might have read this, written exactly 150 years before the crash, discussing an economic crisis in Britain, the USA and northern Europe caused by, in the words of a contemporary parliamentary investigation "excessive speculation and abuse of credit" of all things:

> "What are the social circumstances reproducing, almost regularly, these seasons of self-delusion, of over-speculation and fictitious credit? If they were once traced out, we should arrive at a very plain alternative. Either they may be controlled by society, or they are inherent in the present system of production…"

And as for those disquieted investigators of the 1858 slump he wrote that "…they treat every new crisis as an insulated phenomenon, appearing for the first time on the social horizon and, therefore, by incidents, movements and agencies altogether peculiar, or presumed to be peculiar, to the one period just elapsed between the penultimate and the ultimate revulsion. If natural philosophers had proceeded by the same puerile method, the world would be taken by surprise on the reappearance even of a comet." [27]

Plus ca change. Surprised is what they were once more in 2008. Society at large has demanded answers for the crash, and been largely disappointed since the political elite seems utterly incapable of rustling any up, since "inherent in the present system of production" was an idea simply beyond their ken. But when the Queen demanded an answer that was of course a much more pressing matter, and she has had better luck. On a tour of the London School of Economics, providentially arranged for just a month or two after the financial storm had broken, Her Majesty made so bold as to ask her hosts how it came to pass that so many clever people in the economic profession had missed the obvious. No immediate reply could be made to the regal inquiry. After some months humming and hawing, however, the cream of British economists finally mustered a response. It was "a failure of the collective imagination of many bright people". [28]

If a dearth of imagination amongst the brightest economists was the best that the Queen could get out of the experts, what hope for the rest of the world? Many of those who rushed to buy a copy of *Capital* or the *Communist Manifesto* as the banks tottered and fell across the USA and Britain may have come away somewhat disappointed if they expected to find therein a ready-made description of economic crisis immediately applicable to the circumstances of 2008-2010.

In fact, a neat description of the events leading up to the 2008 crash can be found in the relatively unread, dry-as-dust wastes of volume two of Marx's masterpiece where, with the editorial assistance of Frederick Engels, we can read this formulation: "The production process appears simply as an unavoidable middle term, a necessary evil for the purpose of money-making. (This explains why all nations characterised by the capitalist mode of production are periodically seized by fits of giddiness in which they try to accomplish the money-making without the mediation of the production process.)" Enough "collective imagination" there, 125 years ahead of time. [29]

As "fits of giddiness" go, the years stretching from the end of the Cold War to the great crash were Olympic-class. One measure of it is that between 1990 and 2004 the average time an investor held on to a particular stock shrunk from just over two years to just six months. World debt levels doubled between 2002 and the crash in 2008, to $195 trillion. And here is a contemporary hedge fund king, Kenneth Griffin of Chicago-based Citadel LLC braying in 2015 "I don't manufacture cars, but we do manufacture money", the dream of the bourgeois down the ages. [30]

In the words of economists Ben Fine and Alfred Saad-Filho the underlying cause of crisis is "the subordination of the production of use values to the production of surplus value" expressed through disproportionality, over-production, under-consumption and a falling rate of profit, or the contradiction between social production and private appropriation. That would seem to cover everything, more or less. The pithy summary of course conceals a wealth of controversy among Marxists as to the cause of crisis in general. However, most Marxists would probably give a starring role in the present slump to the idea of an over-accumulation of capital, driven at root by a massive increase in wage labour, and hence surplus value, worldwide, occasioned in turn by the restoration of capitalism in half of Europe and the still more important incorporation of China and India's millions of workers into the world commodity-producing economy. Alan Greenspan, in the days when he was still an oracle, testified to US Congress to the rejuvenating effect a billion new wage-labourers was having on the world capitalist economy. Phillip Coggan summarised it thus: "...the arrival of China and then the former Soviet Union and its satellites into the capitalist world at a stroke...added hundreds of millions of workers to the available labour force. This ensured that wages in the western world were under steady downward pressure.." and, he could have added, that profits would soar. [31]

This historic transformation, making wage-labour the global norm for the first time ever, had started to pile up capital which, all dressed up but with no place to go, could not easily be reinvested at a rate which maintained the prevailing rate of profit. In Arrighi's words "the investment of an every-growing mass of profits in trade and production inevitably leads to the accumulation of capital over and above what can be reinvested in the purchase and sale of commodities without drastically reducing profit margins." Hence the attraction of the ever-growing pyramid of expanding claims on the real economy – the spliced-and-diced debt instruments above all - offering safe, rapid and endless returns at a mouth-watering rate. Only they didn't, of course. [32]

Instead of attending to the danger of an imminent collapse of this tower of speculative froth, the masters of the universe were listening to the likes of Gordon Brown, a buttoned-down man, and about as given to emotional expression as his predecessor as British Prime Minister was to self-doubt. But he really loved the City of London, which he served as Chancellor of the Exchequer for ten years.

Thus in 2007, as the first tremors of the great credit crunch were already discernible, he told a City audience: "Over the ten years that I have had the privilege of addressing you as Chancellor, I have been able year by year to record how the City of London has risen by your efforts, ingenuity and creativity to become a new world leader...an era that history will record as the beginning of a new golden age for the City of London. The financial services sector in Britain, and the City of London at the centre of it, is a great example of a highly skilled, high value added, talent driven industry that shows how we can excel in a world of global competition. Britain needs more of the vigour, ingenuity and aspiration that you already demonstrate..." [33]

Clearly, Britain didn't need any such thing. And while it may be rash to pre-empt history's measured judgements, it seems fairly certain that "golden age" is not how the activities of high finance in the first part of this century will be recorded. Perhaps some of Brown's 2007 audience knew that the game was almost up even then. Certainly a few bank chiefs were smarter than the politicians who grotesquely fawned on them and facilitated their speculation. Jamie Dimon, chief of J.P.Morgan, had observed that "no-one has the right to not assume that the business cycle will turn". He showed more awareness of the rhythms of economic history than the soon-to-be Prime Minister (and rapidly after ex-Prime Minister) of Britain. [34]

For the most part, however, the elite was less concerned with explaining what had happened to the economy than they were with worrying about the potential political repercussions. Here, from the *Financial Times* in 2006, at the dizzy apex of the neo-liberal euphoria, is a summary of politics as it should be for the establishment: "...the intellectual victory of capitalism...has deprived the political elites of independent power and placed them in the service of financial markets." Politicians of that time were expected to look after elite interests above all. "...the ultimate demonstration of solidarity to the 'international community' would be to do what the international community wants even in the face of massive resistance from your domestic political constituency", Paul Krugman wrote. Davos trumps democracy! [35] But there was a new and baffling reality for the *Financial Times* in 2010: "The return of politics is one more cause for concern...Over the past couple of decades political risk has not been something investors have had to really worry about. Markets have been driven by light-touch regulation, laissez-faire economic policies and globalisation rather than by politicians. All that has changed....politicians are already making their presence felt and with mainly negative consequences for markets." [36]

Most politicians have, it should be said, wallowed in their disempowerment. Their trade has transmuted into bailiff and steward for the wealthiest, for high finance and the biggest business. Their managerial role discharged to the latter's satisfaction, they have eased themselves, Labour and Tory, social democratic and liberal, Democrat and Republican, into boardroom sinecures, as rewards for their passivity and lack of initiative when in office. It is perhaps the only profession where doing little or nothing at work is now the guarantee of ever better-paid employment down the line. The New Labour government of Blair and Brown presents a particularly dismal spectacle, as one Cabinet member after another, led by Blair himself of course, have enlisted in the direct and paid service of big business immediately on leaving government, moving onto the boardrooms of banks and the boudoirs of despots (the Murdoch boudoir among them, of course).

So what do the financial-page pundits mean when they worry about the end of the happy days when apolitical politicians could openly fawn on the greediest capitalists, and spout nonsense to their heart's content, and about the "return of politics"? First of all, a return of democratic choices, under which a change of government might mean a change of public policy – the election of Syriza in Greece early in 2015 perhaps embodies "political risk" in this respect, although not much as it turned out. Secondly, a more general rebirth of the concept of "class struggle", of the idea that different parts of society have different interests, that they might actively contest economic and social decision-making across the board, and that different ways of organising society as a whole might be considered as options. Finally, that international conflict might return, burying the rose-tinted bromides of a pacific "new world order".

That order is under strain on almost every front. Despite continuing to display an awesome amount of military power in the region, the US has failed to impose an amenable (to itself) new settlement on the Middle East. It has certainly proved capable of helping to destroy one state after another – Iraq, Libya, Syria, Yemen - but it has not been able to put in place a new Pax Americana to ensure control of the region's peoples and resources. Not only Israel but also long-standing Arab allies like Saudi Arabia are tending to follow more self-determined (and entirely reactionary) policies and asserting their own interests regardless of Washington's views. Nor has this led to a better Middle East – instead the region has collapsed into a bloody swamp of sectarian turmoil and regional power conflict as the promise of the Arab Spring is incrementally obliterated, with the western powers doing enough to keep the fighting going in Syria and Iraq, but denying anyone the capacity to end it.

The developing tensions in the Pacific region are, in the longer run, even more threatening. The growing economic power of China has eventually morphed into the capacity for a strategic challenge to the seventy-year hegemony the US has exercised over the Pacific Rim – the centre of the fastest-growing economies in the world. Obama's much-vaunted "pivot to Asia" – meaning the transfer of some of the Pentagon's wherewithal to that theatre – is designed to send a message that hegemony will not be surrendered lightly. China's growing assertiveness in its own home waters has led to mounting friction with several US-allied neighbours, while the increasing bellicose rhetoric from Japanese militarists and conservatives has raised tensions further. More than anywhere else in the world, the Far East displays the symptoms of 1914 in almost classical form, with rising powers coming into conflict with established economic and security structures; mounting bellicose rhetoric over territorial rights and other claims, military manoeuvres to back this up and so on. The clash between China and the established powers has spread elsewhere, too, most notably in a scramble for African resources. China has invested heavily in the continent, while the US has responded by setting up a Pentagon regional command to cover Africa, the only part of the planet not previously blessed with such oversight. And Chinese influence stretches further. In an article highlighting China's growing role in the Ecuadorian economy ($11 billion invested by Chinese banks), the *New York Times* summarised the global challenge thus: "With the centre of financial gravity shifting, China is aggressively asserting its economic clout to win diplomatic allies, invest its vast wealth, promote its currency and secure much-needed natural resources." Assessing China's rise is another book in itself, and it poses a further challenge for those holding fast to every dot and comma of Lenin's theory of imperialism, since China today ticks most of the boxes while eschewing political interference in the states it invests in. "We are trying to replace American imperialism with Chinese imperialism," Alberto Acosta, ex-energy minister in Ecuador's progressive government, has said. Gideon Rachman cites the imperial (and imperialist) historian Niall Ferguson, from the other end of the political spectrum, as warning against the dangers of Chinese imperialism in Africa (not British, French or American of course), seeing in it "a re-run of the early 1900s, with America in the role of Britain and China in the role of Germany". We know how that ended. [37]

In Latin America, too, the US has had its tail tweaked this century. In one country after another, to one extent or another, the people of the traditional "back yard" of US imperialism have set off on a different course, both tackling the gross poverty and inequalities which have always been the hallmark of capitalism across Latin America and also asserting a new independence in international affairs. Not coincidentally, Russia's actions over Ukraine have found a far more sympathetic hearing in the south of the American continent than in the north. The US has pushed back, of course, against the Chavez-led "Bolivarian revolution" in Venezuela in particular. In Honduras and Paraguay, left-wing governments have been forced from office by elite power backed by the US, even as Washington has been forced to finally come to terms with the Communist government in Cuba, after more than fifty years of futile hostility.

This all paints a picture of declining US power. Here a measure of correcting balance may be needed. The decline is relative and, to some extent reversible. Some leading writers on the anti-imperialist left, like Tariq Ali, deny that there has been a decline at all. They do so partly to criticise those who use the argument of US "weakness" to avoid opposing Washington policy at all, or to deny its imperialist essence. They can point, rightly, to the overwhelming weight of US military power deployed around the world, including in the Middle East, where that power is supposed to be on the retreat, and also to the reluctance of elites elsewhere, including in Russia and China, to push opposition to the US beyond a point. Those elites would most likely rather have a super-imperialist USA which would guarantee due consideration for their interest too, rather than have to oppose it flat-out, in the manner of the old Soviet Union. Notwithstanding, some aspects of the relative decline are objective and irreversible short of a cataclysmic war, if then – the rise of China is one such. The discrediting of the "Washington Consensus" economic model is another, although the lack of an articulated alternative leaves it in place for now. Ali dismisses all actual or potential external challenges to US power. "In reality, the imperial highway is unconquered and unconquerable from without; the only serious exit route lies within the country. What combination of social forces at home can defeat the labyrinthine power structures of the United States? However bleak such a vision might appear, there is no other on the horizon." This surely goes too far, in relegating the rest of the world to spectators, waiting on the development of a profound radical movement in the USA which, while certainly desirable, does not seem on the horizon at present, at least on the scale required. [38]

What is little appreciated in Washington itself is that for much of the world a relative decline in the capacity of the US to do as it pleases is a matter for considerable rejoicing. When Russia brushed aside Georgia's offensive in 2008, humiliating a government in Tiblisi that was a sort of neo-con international with ministers drawn from US, British and Israeli backgrounds and in some cases continuing citizenship, most of Asia, the Middle East and Latin America cheered, not so much from an infatuation with Vladimir Putin as from a delight that the US has received a bloody nose-by-proxy.

As Singapore's former Ambassador to the United Nations Kishore Mahbubani observed at the time:

> "...most of the world is bemused by western moralising on Georgia. America would not tolerate Russia intruding into its geopolitical sphere in Latin America. Hence Latin Americans see American double standards clearly. So do all the Muslim commentaries note that the US invaded Iraq illegally, too. Neither India nor China is moved to protest against Russia. It shows how isolated is the western view on Georgia: that the world should support the underdog, Georgia, against Russia. In reality, most support Russia against the bullying west. The gap between the western narrative and the rest of the world could not be greater." [39]

The right of reading the last rites over the departing hegemony should go to Francis Fukuyama, the end-of-history man himself. Swapping the dialectics of 19th century German philosophy for the rhetoric of 21st century Madison Avenue, he surveyed the wreckage of the two big ideas – "unfettered capitalism" and the "export of democracy" and pronounced: "...a more intangible, yet potentially much greater cost to the United States [is] the damage that the financial meltdown is doing to America's 'brand'." [40]

So could "brand-promotion" – the need for the tarnished world order to restore its momentum through a decisive victory over all alternatives in a key country – have contributed to the Ukraine crisis? Certainly the experience of the twentieth century is that economic dislocation and slump make such conflicts more not less likely, as a gain for one power in a shrinking world market becomes a loss for another. When the opportunities for super-profit become more limited, the recourse to coercion becomes a more attractive option. And US neo-Conservatism has clearly made not "losing" Ukraine its new litmus test for maintaining the "greatness" of the USA itself.

Britain and the New Order

Britain's aggressive role in the Ukrainian crisis has been conditioned by its place in the general imperial world order, and by its own related peculiarities as an imperialist power.

The ruling element of British capital is without doubt the City of London, or the "financial services" sector. As a world financial centre, the City rivals New York, while being attached to a much smaller national economy of course - a national economy to which it accords scant priority in any case. Its vision is global, its scope for money-making as unbounded as it was in the high days of Empire. This gives the City and the British elite a vested interest in a well-policed world, where neither states nor non-state actors are allowed any scope for disrupting the accumulation of capital across the world, in which the City plays the most central part. Policing requires a policeman, and Britain itself no longer fits the part. It can and does play host to the hottest of hot money, offer low- or no-tax refuge to the oligarchs of the east and the princelings of the Gulf alike, but it cannot unaided reach out and protect them and their loot in their own lands. For that a mightier power is required, but one which sometimes needs prompting as to how it should conduct itself. Jim Callaghan is reputed to have told Henry Kissinger at the height of the 1974 Cyprus crisis "you provide the muscle Henry, and we'll provide the brains." Margaret Thatcher told the first President Bush "don't go wobbly George" when it momentarily looked as if Washington might not go to war over Kuwait in 1991. Tony Blair put it uncharacteristically honestly when he said Britain, or British soldiers to be exact, must sometimes "pay a blood price" for maintaining the all-important united front with the USA. They were all expressing the same thing – British capitalism's place in the world order depends on not only keeping in with Washington, but also ensuring that it follows a strategy of keeping the world open for business – that the "hidden fist" which keeps the world safe for the "hidden hand of the market", in *New York Times* journalist Thomas Friedman's memorable phrase, "the hidden fist that ...is called the US Army, Air Force, Navy and Marine Corps" does not stay unduly hidden in practice.

Sometimes that means leading from the front. It was David Cameron and French President Nicholas Sarkozy who took the initiative in attacking Libya in 2011, a conflict which has had catastrophic consequences which reverberate to this day. Sarkozy acted at the prompting of the fatuous philosopher Bernard-Henry Levy (who has also given himself a starring role in the agitation around Ukraine, seeking no doubt to replicate his Libyan "triumph" in eastern Europe); Cameron as a pragmatic British Tory surely determined his policy without reference to anything or anyone so continental. Again, it was Cameron (this time with Sarkozy's social democratic successor Francois Hollande in the Elysee) who tried to start war with Syria in 2013 while President Obama appeared quite relieved to wriggle out from an attack following the voting down of Cameron's project in the British House of Commons.

This does not mean that Britain simply functions as Washington's puppet. Indeed, its scope for independent initiative seems to have increased under Cameron. As with other Washington allies, it has taken to moving on its own account when Obama has hesitated. This is of course circumscribed by several factors, not least the relative lack of funds for unbridled war-making. The City wants the world protecting for profit, but it doesn't want its own profits taxed sufficient to pay for that protection. Efforts by the right-wing in politics and the media to ramp up British arms spending appear to be bearing fruit, but not to the point where gunboat diplomacy becomes a viable option once more.

City ambivalence about the consequences of being a cornerstone in a united imperialist front were further displayed in the early days of the Ukraine crisis when Cameron advisers, doubtless prompted by the City, where seen carrying position papers ruling out any response to the Crimean annexation which might curb the flood of Russian money, much of it doubtless illicitly secured, pouring into British-based financial institutions. This, however, proved to be a passing sectional concern within the British elite, as opposed to the strategic imperative of confronting Putin in the interests of the "world order" as a whole.

Returning to the underlying basis of imperialism – the search for super-profit and the maintenance of a world order ensuring higher profits for the centres of global capitalism - it is easy to see why the British state would still play a critical role. The key centres of imperialist power – the financial system and its monopolist banks, the oil industry and other energy transnational companies and the arms manufacturers are all central to the British ruling class today. All have interests in the expansionist policies pursued by NATO and the EU in Eastern Europe, enthusiastically backed by successive British governments. All help address one of the already-noted central difficulties of monopoly capitalism – the absorption of surplus capital. As Lapavitsas writes "the normal state of the monopolistic capitalist economy is to be overwhelmed by surplus. It follows that methods must emerge through which the surplus would be absorbed, either in production or in consumption". [41]

Take the arms industry as an example of how this is done. It is a sector of which the role as an outlet for investing surplus capital is most pronounced in the USA, Britain and France, the three leading aggressor powers in world politics this century (notwithstanding France's abstention from the Iraq War). The biggest companies of the arms industry enlist the services of the home state at one end and often corrupt functionaries of the purchasing state at the other to ensure markets which yield fantastic profits and, at the price of war scares and conjured up threats, takes huge quantities of surplus capital out of circulation whether or not the arms are ever actually used. Here is state-guaranteed super-profit.

It is small surprise that the "defence" industry retains huge political leverage in the great powers, even in a time of military budgets reduced somewhat from their Cold War peaks. The conglomerate now known as BAE Systems, not only Britain's biggest defence company but its biggest manufacturing corporation of any type, has long enjoyed access to Downing Street rivalled only, perhaps, by that of BP. This is not only because politicians obviously control the size and distribution of their own country's defence budget. There is also the indispensable role of the state in authorising external arms sales, which has long since passed over into the task of actually helping sell them.

This is where the state and monopoly capital fuse most closely. Arms spending has particular advantages for the system as a whole, as Rosa Luxemburg pointed out long ago:

> "In the form of government contracts for army supplies the scattered purchasing power of the consumers is concentrated in large quantities and, free from the vagaries and subjective fluctuations of personal consumption, it achieves an almost automatic regularity and rhythmic growth. Capital itself ultimately controls this automatic and rhythmic movement of militarist production through the legislature and a press whose function is to mould so-called 'public opinion'. That is why this particular province of capitalist accumulation at first seems capable of infinite expansion...production for militarism represents a province whose regular and progressive expansion seems primarily determined by capital itself." [42]

Britain under the "new Labour" government provided egregious examples to support Luxemburg's case. Tony Blair flew to India in 2002 to clinch a one billion pound arms deal while the purchaser and its neighbour, Pakistan, were still not far from the brink of open conflict. British taxpayers' money was, of course, used to grease the transaction. Blair also backed a £28 million arms transaction with Tanzania which even his own development and aid officials said was utterly unnecessary. The choice between what Africa needed and what military monopolies wanted did not appear to detain him for long. The story of the Labour government closing down a police enquiry into the allegations of corruption surrounding BAe's multi-billion weapons sales to the Saudi Arabian kleptocracy in order to save the former's business while sparing the latter's blushes is well known. "Arms sales," according to former Cabinet member Clare Short, were "Tony's blind spot." Among several others, it might be added. David Cameron has been no more far-sighted, acquiescing in Saudi aggression against Bahrain and Yemen, not to mention its role in promoting the most reactionary variants of Islam, in part because of its reliability as a buyer of British munitions – a point made explicit by Tory Foreign Secretary Phillip Hammond in endorsing Riyadh's 2015 attack on Yemen. This is an area where front-bench bipartisan harmony prevails without interruption, as it does with most questions touching upon imperialism, a fact which made Ed Miliband's resistance to the planned Anglo-American air strike against Syria such a remarkable and significant event. [43]

Britain is, some years at least, the biggest arms exporter in the world, accounting for fully one-third of the total trade (with a huge slice of the business being transacted in the Middle East, of course). In a good year for arms companies the arms trade contributes almost as much as "financial services" to the British economy. [44]

Here is a single story which outlines how coercion and super-profit, state and "market" work in today's world: In the immediate aftermath of the Iraq invasion, the British arms industry felt it wasn't getting a fair crack of the whip from the Pentagon weapons buyers. The British Defence Procurement Minister of the time, one Lord Bach, complained: "UK servicemen are putting their lives on the line and everybody knows that the Prime Minister took a huge political risk. It is astonishing that we can work so intimately with the Americans, yet in the field of defence industry co-operation we are treated in such a way." Still more explicitly, another Defence Ministry source told the *Observer*: "Our soldiers are out there being killed alongside GIs, and we are treated no better than Belgium." So what were we fighting for in Iraq then? In order that our arms salesmen are not treated like Belgians when they knock at the door of the Pentagon, apparently. Small surprise that many military families took to protesting against the war, including bereaved parents, in an unprecedented political development. [45]

The death and maiming of their children bore fruit as intended by those who sent them to Iraq. British Aerospace profits had risen to a considerably improved £643 million by the first half of 2007 – "massively exceeding market expectation" according to one analyst. The company attributed this to the "high tempo" of Anglo-US wars in Afghanistan and Iraq, and consequently "numerous urgent operational requirement orders" from the Pentagon above all. It is fair to assume the company has been depressed by the diminished "tempo" of those two conflicts, and quite anxious to see others take their place. Annual profits remain at roughly the 2007 level, but there is hope, the company's chief executive reported when announcing 2014 results: "We continue to win significant new business with over £10bn of new orders from the UK and US for the third successive year…Looking ahead, defence spending remains a high priority in a number of international markets. In the UK, we benefit from long-term contracts, notwithstanding continued pressure on public spending." [46]

Lord Bach's evident misery on behalf of the British arms monopolies, and BAE's happy report that his Lordship could go easy on himself now, also point the way towards another important mutation in the world economy – the increasing industrial power of the Pentagon (hence the US government) and its ability to restructure big business in the manufacturing and high-tech sectors, an example of burgeoning super-imperialism at work. Its weapon here is access to the vast US arms budget, which it can use to control corporate policy. One example of this was the suggestion that BAE might relocate to the USA, and become in effect an "American" firm in order to increase its access to Washington's military budget, non-US firms being restricted to bidding for contracts worth at most two per cent of the 644 billion dollar total. [47]

None of this excludes rivalry between the big powers in this field, too. For example, it seems that one motive behind France's enthusiasm for war against Libya in 2011 was the desire to win markets, including arms orders, from US and British companies in the Middle East. E-mails released in the US have revealed that the preposterous philosopher Bernard-Henri Levy, whose role has already been mentioned, had arranged for the French action to secure regime change in Libya he advocated to be accompanied by guarantees that a post-Gaddafi government would favour French business interests, particularly in the oil and arms industries. Then-President Sarkozy demanded 35% of the oil industry for French firms as the price for his "humanitarian" intervention. French arms sales in the region have risen 42% since the war, and are going still higher. Levy, fresh from brokering this deal, has taken his philosophical talents eastwards, appearing in Maidan to denounce the Russian government. Who know what benefits will accrue to the giant monopolies of France as a result? [48]

So the huge arms companies become on the one hand more closely entwined with "their own" national states and politicians, while on the other reconfiguring into a global elite centred on the United States and its military-industrial interests. It is ironic that the main area in which the US still enjoys a competitive advantage is the one area, militarism, wherein, as Luxemburg noted, the all-holy "rules of the market" barely apply, and are distorted at every turn by politics, state intervention and officially-sanctioned corruption. An "endless war" against media-manufactured phantom enemies naturally provides exceptional opportunities for the continued levying of this form of super-profit. Putin has thus been made into a god-send for the arms-makers and arms traders of the world. And no wonder the IMF will not hear a word said against arms spending, the only form of state expenditure it has learned to love.

"We are all Americans Now" was the cry from the heart given banner headlines in *Le Monde* in solidarity with the people of the USA after 9/11. It is the cry from the wallet of the arms manufacturers of much of the world, Britain not least. It was also, ironically, the position taken up by the Russian government at the time, facilitating US operations in Afghanistan, to the extent of not obstructing the establishment of US bases in the former Soviet republic of Kirghizia. Small thanks Moscow got for it.

What is true of the arms companies is just as true of the energy giants. BP, like BAe has had an open door into government. It is as cosy with Westminster and Whitehall as Gazprom is with the Kremlin, even if the connections are somewhat more discreetly veiled. And although BP likes to play down its "British" foundations the better to play up its global role, it is to the British state that it turns for diplomatic assistance and more in a crisis, most recently in relation to the Deepwater Horizon oil spill in the Gulf of Mexico. Again, this is because state intervention and support is an avenue to super-profit. Such companies do not prosper in the free market – the state is their helpmate at every turn. These considerations all come together in the unconditional support given by the British government to the autocracies of the Gulf, including Saudi Arabia above all. Not only do these regimes owe their wealth to oil, they then obligingly spend some of it on arms purchases and deposit much of the rest with the City to invest – or simply launder. The Gulf elites are now at the core of the establishment in Britain.

So British imperialism is not a matter of history alone. The main drivers of imperialist policy – the largest banks and financial institutions at the centre of the world system of speculation, energy companies dependent on access to key resources and military monopolies who thrive on international tension and ultimately war – carry decisive weight in the counsels of state.

But nor does this mean nothing has changed. In all these areas there has been a metamorphosis in the direction of an Anglo-American imperial alliance, "an Anglo-Saxon world imperialism", a development first foreseen by Communist International economist Eugene Varga ninety years ago. US banks occupy decisive positions in the City and, as noted, British-headquartered arms and energy monopolies do as much or more of their business in or through the USA. Britain's leading role in NATO but more equivocal attitude towards the EU reflects this.

As noted already, the absence of the British Empire from any list of world powers is the most obvious change in world power centres over the course of the twentieth century. But the nature of British monopoly capital ensures that it will likely be at the centre of any major international conflict in the twenty-first. [49]

Russia and the Ukrainian Mirror

All these currents – the instability of the post-1991 world system, the eastward drive of NATO and the EU, the effects of the economic crisis on the search for monopoly profits - in world affairs have come together in the Ukraine crisis. In Britain and elsewhere in the west, it has been seen mainly through the same shop-worn narrative as is deployed for every such crisis – foreign dictator, unfathomable aggression, the west all too reasonable for its own good, strong response needed, no parallels at all with western behaviour elsewhere, and so on. Millions of people around the world see the post-1991 system, and the conflicts which have marked it, differently.

There have, of course, been different views within the establishments of the NATO/EU bloc. They were summed up by an outraged Philip Stephens, the consistently bellicose political columnist for the *Financial Times*, thus: "Italy's policy towards Russia has often seemed to be written by the energy group ENI...French defence companies have lucrative contracts to worry about, while Britain's BP is concerned about losing hefty dividends from its Russian energy interests. Then there are the London-based financial institutions who wash and press Russian roubles." [50]

And that was without even mentioning Germany. Former Chancellor Gerhard Schroeder has been consistently pro-Putin, as might be expected from a man with a seat on the board of Gazprom. Germany exports around 35 billion Euros-worth of machinery, equipment and chemicals to Russia, a consideration which doubtless led the Director-General of the Federation of German Industries, Markus Kerber, to declare that "German industry is neither Russophile nor Russophobe. It is our responsibility to help end this confrontation."

Nevertheless, these voices have not set the tone for the western response to the Ukrainian crisis, just as concerns for keeping Russian money in the City of London have not noticeably moderated Britain's position. Even if public opinion has not swung behind their leaders' pumped-up rhetoric, it has broadly accepted the official narrative concerning the goodies and baddies in Ukraine. The alternative view has had little or no hearing in the west.

This "alternative" outlook was summed up by President Putin in his address to the Russian Duma proposing the formal annexation of the Crimea in March 2014. It is cited at length (and will be again later on in relation to directly Ukrainian questions) because it encapsulates this different perspective, not just on Ukraine but on the entire cast of world politics this century to date. Although ridiculed by liberal Anglo-American punditry, it is unlikely that more than a handful of world leaders outside the NATO bloc would disagree with a word of it:

> "Like a mirror, the situation in Ukraine reflects what is going on and what has been happening in the world over the past several decades. After the dissolution of bipolarity on the planet, we no longer have stability. Key international institutions are not getting any stronger; on the contrary, in many cases, they are sadly degrading. Our western partners, led by the United States of America, prefer not to be guided by international law in their practical policies, but by the rule of the gun. They have come to believe in their exclusivity and exceptionalism, that they can decide the destinies of the world, that only they can ever be right. They act as they please: here and there, they use force against sovereign states, building coalitions based on the principle 'if you are not with us, you are against us.' To make this aggression look legitimate, they force the necessary resolutions from international organisations, and if for some reason this does not work, they simply ignore the UN Security Council and the UN overall.
>
> "This happened in Yugoslavia; we remember 1999 very well. It was hard to believe, even seeing it with my own eyes, that at the end of the 20th century, one of Europe's capitals, Belgrade, was under missile attack for several weeks, and then came the real intervention. Was there a UN Security Council resolution on this matter, allowing for these actions? Nothing of the sort. And then, they hit Afghanistan, Iraq, and frankly violated the UN Security Council resolution on Libya, when instead of imposing the so-called no-fly zone over it they started bombing it too.
>
> "There was a whole series of controlled 'colour' revolutions. Clearly, the people in those nations, where these events took place, were sick of tyranny and poverty, of their lack of prospects; but these feelings were taken advantage of cynically. Standards were imposed on these nations that did not in any way correspond to their way of life, traditions, or these peoples' cultures. As a result, instead of democracy and freedom, there was chaos, outbreaks in violence and a series of upheavals. The Arab Spring turned into the Arab Winter.
>
> "A similar situation unfolded in Ukraine. In 2004, to push the necessary candidate through at the presidential elections, they thought up some sort of third round that was not stipulated by the law. It was absurd and a mockery of the constitution. And now, they have thrown in an organised and well-equipped army of militants.
>
> "We understand what is happening; we understand that these actions were aimed against Ukraine and Russia and against Eurasian integration. And all this while Russia strived to engage in dialogue with our colleagues in the West. We are constantly proposing cooperation on all key issues; we want to strengthen our level of trust and for

our relations to be equal, open and fair. But we saw no reciprocal steps.

"On the contrary, they have lied to us many times, made decisions behind our backs, placed us before an accomplished fact. This happened with NATO's expansion to the East, as well as the deployment of military infrastructure at our borders. They kept telling us the same thing: 'Well, this does not concern you.' That's easy to say.

"It happened with the deployment of a missile defence system. In spite of all our apprehensions, the project is working and moving forward. It happened with the endless foot-dragging in the talks on visa issues, promises of fair competition and free access to global markets.

"Today, we are being threatened with sanctions, but we already experience many limitations, ones that are quite significant for us, our economy and our nation. For example, still during the times of the Cold War, the US and subsequently other nations restricted a large list of technologies and equipment from being sold to the USSR... Today, they have formally been eliminated, but only formally; and in reality, many limitations are still in effect.

"In short, we have every reason to assume that the infamous policy of containment, followed in the 18th, 19th and 20th centuries, continues today. They are constantly trying to sweep us into a corner because we have an independent position, because we maintain it and because we call things like they are and do not engage in hypocrisy. But there is a limit to everything. And with Ukraine, our western partners have crossed the line, playing the bear and acting irresponsibly and unprofessionally.

"After all, they were fully aware that there are millions of Russians living in Ukraine and in Crimea. They must have really lacked political instinct and common sense not to foresee all the consequences of their actions. Russia found itself in a position it could not retreat from. If you compress the spring all the way to its limit, it will snap back hard. You must always remember this." [51]

A reasonable reading of this indicates that Putin is scarcely driven by firm opposition to the USA per se. Instead, he urges the consistent application of the same rules for all powers; an end to unilateral US interventions in countries which Russia itself has an interest in; and a dismantling of remaining cold war measures directed against Russian business. And, of course, Putin's observations bypass Russia's own, small-scale, toe-in-the-water imperial initiatives around its own periphery. These were not the remarks of a tribune of the oppressed, more of a jilted lover.

Putin certainly put his finger on the core of the problem, however. US policy, expressed both in its own actions and through NATO, the European Union and other institutions, has been "compressing the spring" all century, seeking to curb and contain the possible emergence of any rival centre of power or authority on the planet. In Ukraine, the snap back has been hard – hard enough to raise the prospect of war. Putin's point is the same as the one made by British economist Andrew Gamble: "If there is now a retreat not just from globalisation but also from global governance, and from the attempt to forge international agreements, then the risk of other ways being used to settle disputes grows." Since there is, and can be given the present distribution of world power, no possibility of "global governance" , and since even the idea of "same rules for all" is entirely unacceptable to US and British imperialism, "other ways" become more and more likely. [52]

NOTES
1. see Lenin; Hilferding; Bukharin; Hobson
2. Donald, p. 210
3. Lenin p. 25; Marx 1975, p. 140
4. Lenin, pp 26, 123
5. Day p. 115
6. see Murray, 2009; Foreign Policy May 25 2015, *The Atlantic* April 2014
7. Kiernan p. xv
8. Lenin, pp 113, 120
9. Lapavitsas pp 42, 66
10. Bukharin, p. 14
11. see Hardt/Negri; see Screpanti for theory of "global imperialism"
12. Mandel p. 84
13. Boron, p. 123
14. Boron, p. 45; Faux p. 76
15. *Guardian* February 21 2003
16. Wood, p. 6; Boron, p. 8
17. Sakwa, p. 5
18. http://www.nytimes.com/1992/03/08/world/excerpts-from-pentagon-s-plan-prevent-the-re-emergence-of-a-new-rival.html?pagewanted=2
19. Rubio in *Wall Street Journal* August 4 2015; see Perry Anderson in *New Left Review* July/August 2015
20. see www.nationofchange.org
21. *Wall Street Journal*, 10-12 April 2015
22. *Financial Times*, July 15 2015
23. Day, p. 103
24. *Newsweek*, October 13 2008
25. *Financial Times*, October 10 2008
26. Rachman, p. 191
27. Marx 2007 pp 200-204
28. David Smith, p. 207
29. Marx, 1978 p. 137, words in brackets added by Engels
30. Reich, p 71; *Wall Street Journal*, August 5 2015
31. Fine etc, p. 82; Coggan, p. 165
32. Arrighi p. 232
33. David Smith p. 69
34. Tett p.133
35. Hywel Williams, *Financial Times* March 21 2006; Krugman p. 88
36. Neil Hume, *Financial Times* February 6 2010
37. *New York Times*, July 24, 2015; Rachman p. 266
38. Ali, p. 141
39. *Financial Times*, August 21 2008
40. Newsweek, October 13 2008
41. Lapavitsas, p.8
42. Luxemburg, p. 446
43. Porteous, p 127

44 supplement to The Independent, July 2007; UK Trade and Investment press release, June 17 2008
45 *Observer* April 13 2003
46 *Guardian* August 10 2008; http://www.baesystems.com/article/BAES_179438/2014-full-year-results
47 see *Wall Street Journal* 24 August 1999; *The Economist* October 6 2001
48 http://www.nationofchange.org/2015/07/13/ripped-from-hillarys-emails-french-plot-to-overthrow-gaddafi-and-help-itself-to-libyas-oil/
49 Day, p. 69
50 *Financial Times* 17 April 2014
51 http://www.washingtonpost.com/world/transcript-putin-says-russia-will-protect-the-rights-of-russians-abroad/2014/03/18/432a1e60-ae99-11e3-a49e-76adc9210f19_story.html
52 Gamble, p. 165

PART TWO
The Ukraine in five questions

Why?

TO START NEAR the end....Russian president Vladimir Putin set out his view of the crisis in the neighbouring state in the Duma speech already cited (it may be the most significant he has ever made). It outlines a narrative, not just of the immediate triggers for the Maidan movement and the subsequent turmoil, but for the entire unfolding drama of the post-Soviet years from the Russian perspective (and not just that of its ruling elite). He was speaking after the Yanukovych government had been brought down by a combination of street pressure and US interference with the loss of around 100 lives in Kiev, the blame for which is to some extent disputed, and Moscow had acted to annex the Crimean peninsula, following a referendum which, while likewise disputed, undoubtedly expressed a popular majority there for union with Russia. Here, he sets these events in a Russian perspective:

> "Unfortunately, what seemed impossible became a reality. The USSR fell apart. Things developed so swiftly that few people realised how truly dramatic those events and their consequences would be. Many people both in Russia and in Ukraine, as well as in other republics hoped that the Commonwealth of Independent States that was created at the time would become the new common form of statehood. They were told that there would be a single currency, a single economic space, joint armed forces; however, all this remained empty promises, while the big country was gone. It was only when Crimea ended up as part of a different country that Russia realised that it was not simply robbed, it was plundered.
>
> "At the same time, we have to admit that by launching the sovereignty parade Russia itself aided in the collapse of the Soviet Union. And as this collapse was legalised, everyone forgot about Crimea and Sevastopol – the main base of the Black Sea Fleet. Millions of people went to bed in one country and awoke in different ones, overnight becoming ethnic minorities in former Union republics, while the Russian nation became one of the biggest, if not the biggest ethnic group in the world to be divided by borders.
>
> "Now, many years later, I heard residents of Crimea say that back in 1991 they were handed over like a sack of potatoes. This is hard to disagree with. And what about the Russian state? What about Russia? It humbly accepted the situation. This country was going through such hard times then that realistically it was incapable of protecting its interests. However, the people could not reconcile themselves to this outrageous historical injustice. All these years, citizens and many public figures came back to this issue, saying that Crimea is historically Russian land and Sevastopol is a Russian city. Yes, we all knew this in our hearts and minds, but we had to proceed from the existing reality and build our good-neighbourly relations with independent Ukraine on a new basis. Meanwhile, our relations with Ukraine, with the fraternal Ukrainian people have always been and will remain of foremost importance for us.
>
> "Today we can speak about it openly, and I would like to share with you some details

of the negotiations that took place in the early 2000s. The then President of Ukraine Mr Kuchma asked me to expedite the process of delimiting the Russian-Ukrainian border. At that time, the process was practically at a standstill. Russia seemed to have recognised Crimea as part of Ukraine, but there were no negotiations on delimiting the borders. Despite the complexity of the situation, I immediately issued instructions to Russian government agencies to speed up their work to document the borders, so that everyone had a clear understanding that by agreeing to delimit the border we admitted de facto and de jure that Crimea was Ukrainian territory, thereby closing the issue. We accommodated Ukraine not only regarding Crimea, but also on such a complicated matter as the maritime boundary in the Sea of Azov and the Kerch Strait. What we proceeded from back then was that good relations with Ukraine matter most for us and they should not fall hostage to deadlock territorial disputes. However, we expected Ukraine to remain our good neighbour, we hoped that Russian citizens and Russian speakers in Ukraine, especially its southeast and Crimea, would live in a friendly, democratic and civilised state that would protect their rights in line with the norms of international law.

"However, this is not how the situation developed. Time and time again attempts were made to deprive Russians of their historical memory, even of their language and to subject them to forced assimilation. Moreover, Russians, just as other citizens of Ukraine are suffering from the constant political and state crisis that has been rocking the country for over 20 years.

"I understand why Ukrainian people wanted change. They have had enough of the authorities in power during the years of Ukraine's independence. Presidents, prime ministers and parliamentarians changed, but their attitude to the country and its people remained the same. They milked the country, fought among themselves for power, assets and cash flows and did not care much about the ordinary people. They did not wonder why it was that millions of Ukrainian citizens saw no prospects at home and went to other countries to work as day labourers. I would like to stress this: it was not some Silicon Valley they fled to, but to become day labourers. Last year alone almost 3 million people found such jobs in Russia. According to some sources, in 2013 their earnings in Russia totalled over $20 billion, which is about 12% of Ukraine's GDP.

"I would like to reiterate that I understand those who came out on Maidan with peaceful slogans against corruption, inefficient state management and poverty. The right to peaceful protest, democratic procedures and elections exist for the sole purpose of replacing the authorities that do not satisfy the people. However, those who stood behind the latest events in Ukraine had a different agenda: they were preparing yet another government takeover; they wanted to seize power and would stop short of nothing. They resorted to terror, murder and riots. Nationalists, neo-Nazis, Russophobes and anti-Semites executed this coup. They continue to set the tone in Ukraine to this day.

"The new so-called authorities began by introducing a draft law to revise the language policy, which was a direct infringement on the rights of ethnic minorities. However, they were immediately 'disciplined' by the foreign sponsors of these so-called politicians. One has to admit that the mentors of these current authorities are smart and know well what such attempts to build a purely Ukrainian state may lead to. The draft law was set aside, but clearly reserved for the future. Hardly any mention is made of this attempt now, probably on the presumption that people have a short memory. Nevertheless, we can all clearly see the intentions of these ideological heirs of Bandera, Hitler's accomplice during World War II.

"It is also obvious that there is no legitimate executive authority in Ukraine now, nobody to talk to. Many government agencies have been taken over by the impostors, but they do not have any control in the country, while they themselves – and I would like to stress this – are often controlled by radicals....

"Those who opposed the coup were immediately threatened with repression. Naturally, the first in line here was Crimea, the Russian-speaking Crimea. In view of this, the residents of Crimea and Sevastopol turned to Russia for help in defending their rights and lives, in preventing the events that were unfolding and are still underway in Kiev, Donetsk, Kharkov and other Ukrainian cities. Naturally, we could not leave this plea unheeded; we could not abandon Crimea and its residents in distress. This would have been betrayal on our part.

"...We had to help create conditions so that the residents of Crimea for the first time in history were able to peacefully express their free will regarding their own future. However, what do we hear from our colleagues in Western Europe and North America? They say we are violating norms of international law. Firstly, it's a good thing that they at least remember that there exists such a thing as international law – better late than never.

"...As it declared independence and decided to hold a referendum, the Supreme Council of Crimea referred to the United Nations Charter, which speaks of the right of nations to self-determination. Incidentally, I would like to remind you that when Ukraine seceded from the USSR it did exactly the same thing, almost word for word. Ukraine used this right, yet the residents of Crimea are denied it. Why is that?

"Moreover, the Crimean authorities referred to the well-known Kosovo precedent – a precedent our western colleagues created with their own hands in a very similar situation, when they agreed that the unilateral separation of Kosovo from Serbia, exactly what Crimea is doing now, was legitimate and did not require any permission from the country's central authorities...

"I do not like to resort to quotes, but in this case, I cannot help it. Here is a quote from another official document: the Written Statement of the United States America of April 17, 2009, submitted to the same UN International Court in connection with the hearings on Kosovo. Again, I quote: 'Declarations of independence may, and often do, violate domestic legislation. However, this does not make them violations of international law.' End of quote. They wrote this, disseminated it all over the world, had everyone agree and now they are outraged. Over what? The actions of Crimean people completely fit in with these instructions, as it were. For some reason, things that Kosovo Albanians (and we have full respect for them) were permitted to do, Russians, Ukrainians and Crimean Tatars in Crimea are not allowed. Again, one wonders why.

"We keep hearing from the United States and Western Europe that Kosovo is some special case. What makes it so special in the eyes of our colleagues? It turns out that it is the fact that the conflict in Kosovo resulted in so many human casualties. Is this a legal argument? The ruling of the International Court says nothing about this. This is not even double standards; this is amazing, primitive, blunt cynicism...according to this logic, we have to make sure every conflict leads to human losses…

"There was not a single armed confrontation in Crimea and no casualties. Why do you think this was so? The answer is simple: because it is very difficult, practically impossible to fight against the will of the people….They keep talking of some Russian intervention in Crimea, some sort of aggression. This is strange to hear. I cannot recall a single case in history of an intervention without a single shot being fired and with no human casualties." [1]

Putin is, of course, an authoritarian whose rule has consolidated oligarchic domination of Russia's economy while squeezing the space for most forms of democratic expression. His opponents have been hounded or imprisoned, as he has justified his rule by an ideological concoction of social conservatism, chauvinism and nostalgia (while scarcely moving to a full-blown dictatorship). Nevertheless, all the main points he makes in the above passage are accurate, and the situation in Ukraine cannot be addressed without acknowledging them:

The 1991 post-Soviet settlement had left a pile of unresolved problems in terms of people finding themselves citizens of states they did not necessarily identify with.

Russia was particularly humiliated as part of this process which, he acknowledges, it had brought upon itself.

The Russian and Ukrainian people shared a deeply entwined common life and heritage, which the 1991 settlement did not acknowledge, the more so since the Commonwealth of Independent States which could have provided a post-Soviet structure proved to be an empty shell.

Since 1991 Ukraine had been chronically misgoverned, and those of its citizens who protested against this should have understanding and support.

Russia had played fair by Ukraine in all bilateral matters since they became separate states.

While Yanukovych could legitimately be opposed and defeated in elections, what happened was an illegitimate seizure of power.

The Maidan movement, whatever its origins, had brought to power an unrepresentative group of virulent Ukrainian nationalists, heirs to neo-fascist movements of the past and strongly hostile to Russia and Russians living in Ukraine.

Under these circumstances the people of Crimea, never terribly happy as part of Ukraine in any case, exercised their right to self-determination and voted to unite with Russia.

NATO's Yugoslav war, which supported Kosova's separation from Serbia, provides a political and legal precedent for such a move.

Had Russia not acceded to Crimea's request, there would have been considerable bloodshed there.

Of course, there are missing aspects from this account. The Russian state was certainly a more proactive in the detaching of Crimea from Ukraine than Putin was prepared to admit at that point, and one of the reasons is not hard to find – the retention of the vast Russian Black Sea Fleet base at Sevastopol on the Crimean peninsula (although technically a separate administrative unit from the wider region, still part of Ukraine).

Nor, indeed, should his rhetoric about protecting Russians in the Ukraine be taken at face value. Subsequent developments in the east of the country support the view that they are to be used as bargaining chips to further Moscow's strategic and commercial interests.

Certainly, referendum votes in Donetsk and Luhansk to declare independence have met with less support than the identical Crimean initiative from official Russia, and Putin's policy reflects both the need to accommodate the nationalist feeling it has helped stimulate as well as elite desires to retain their place in the US-led world system.

But whether one buys the Putin narrative or not, it spells out clearly the main considerations which explain why the issue of which trade agreement Ukraine should sign reached such a boiling point. These should now be examined in greater detail.

Where?

While Ukrainian peoples had occupied most of the lands now covered by the Ukrainian state – along with millions of Russians, Poles, Jews and others – Ukraine as a defined political territory did not exist before the Russian revolution. Nor, with very brief exceptions, did it exist as an independent political entity before 1991 and the collapse of the Soviet Union. The Germans sponsored a Ukrainian state in 1918, after the Treaty of Brest-Litovsk which ended Russian (Soviet) participation in the First World War. This Hetmanate did not survive Germany's own defeat at the end of the year. A slightly more durable Ukrainian National Republic, sponsored by France this time, was established in some of the Ukrainian lands in 1919, but this in turn imploded under Polish pressure from the West and Soviet advance from the east. In the midst of all this a West Ukrainian republic (covering only a fraction of the territory now constituting western Ukraine) lived briefly and died, more under Polish blows than Russian. Finally, the only surviving Ukrainian state form was the Ukrainian Soviet Republic, which created the USSR together with Soviet Russia, Belorussia and the Transcaucasian republics in 1922. However, by then the Soviet-Polish war had led to Poland, itself a newly (re)created state , establishing its power over huge territories with a Ukrainian majority population, including lands drawn from both the Tsarist and Austro-Hungarian empires pre-war. The frontiers established as a result of that conflict lay well to the east of the Curzon Line, the frontier set down by British Foreign Secretary Lord Curzon as constituting the most natural ethnographic border between Soviet/Russian-ruled lands and Poland as could be contrived. This excess of Polish imperialism undermined the foundations of the new Polish state from the start, making of it an oppressor of other peoples even as it constituted its own statehood afresh after a gap of many generations.

The boundaries of contemporary Ukraine are entirely the work of Lenin and Stalin, with one significant exception. The Soviet government set itself the task of uniting all Ukrainian-peopled lands within the boundaries of Soviet Ukraine in the course of the 1939-45 war. This was done piecemeal and, of course, controversially. This process of unification also involved the removal of non-Ukrainian peoples, Poles from western Ukraine most of all – a work of ethnic cleansing largely undertaken by the Bandera Ukrainian fascists during 1944-45, who hoped to create an independent Ukraine, rather than the returning Soviet authorities. Reciprocally, Polish nationalists massacred or deported Ukrainians from their territories at the same time, leaving both states with an ethnic homogeneity never previously experienced (Ukrainian and Polish nationalists, with the occupying Nazis in the lead, destroyed the area's large Jewish population).

The only non-Stalinist initiative, as it were, which shaped post-1991 Ukraine was the transfer of the Crimean peninsula from the Russian to the Ukrainian Soviet Republic in 1954.

This perennially unpopular move was made by Khrushchev, ostensibly to mark the 300th anniversary of the unifying treaty between the two lands but also perhaps to shore up Ukrainian support for his leadership at a difficult time, although there was also a certain geographical and economic rationale. This rearrangement may not have made a great deal of difference at the time, since it was merely a transfer within the state structures of the integral USSR, but it stored up a lot of trouble for the post-Soviet future as it turned out. Even the formal status of Crimea was complicated – the great port city of Sevastopol, home to the Russian Black Sea fleet and site of prolonged heroic resistance to a German siege during the war, was administratively entirely separate from the rest of the peninsula and was dubbed a location of "all-union significance", directly under Moscow's control rather than that of the Kiev authorities. By this time Crimea had been voided of its Tartar population, deported en masse during the war on account of the collaboration of much of its leadership with the German occupation of the peninsula. This act of very rough justice, if it was justice at all, analogous to the mass internment of Japanese-Americans after Pearl Harbour, or the expulsion of the Germans from Sudetenland in Czechoslovakia at war's end, was only reversed in 1989. Today some 300,000 Tartars live in the presently Russian-ruled Crimea.

Comment on contemporary Ukraine often over-simplifies this history, and pits "west" against "east", an obligingly Manichean formula that draws on Cold War language and concepts while also eliding the complex differences in history and culture within, as well as between, these binary divisions.

Western Ukraine, for example, is scarcely an historical unity. Three of the seven provinces in Ukraine's west, constituting the heartland of Ukrainian nationalism – Lviv, Ivanovo-Frankivsk and Ternopil – together constituted the eastern part of Galicia, a Polish-dominated but mainly Ukrainian-populated part of the Austro-Hungarian empire until 1918, ultimately governed from Vienna. After the disintegration of the Empire, and the subsequent Polish-Soviet war, the provinces came under Polish control and were ruled from Warsaw until 1939. So too were the present Ukrainian provinces of Volhynia and Rivne – these were however part of the Tsarist Empire (as Volhynia) and were Russian-ruled until the aftermath of the First World War when they too were incorporated into Pilsudski's Poland.

The present Zakarpattia (Transcarpathia) province also formed part of the Austro-Hungarian lands. It was governed from Budapest however, under the Dual Monarchy system. Ukrainian peasants, like Slovakians, were oppressed by Hungarian gentry. It was incorporated in the new Czechoslovakian state created by the Versailles Treaty (following a somewhat extraordinary referendum conducted among immigrants from the region to the USA, who could not have been affected by the outcome one way or another, but declared for Czechoslovakia nonetheless). The post-Munich dismemberment of Czechoslovakia in 1938-39 saw it returned to Hungarian control – it is often forgotten that Hungary and Poland benefitted from Hitler's destruction of Czechoslovakia, as well of course as the Reich. The province was returned to Prague in 1945, but its people then voted to join Soviet Ukraine the next year. In 1991 they sought autonomy within the independent Ukraine, but were not given it. Support for Ukrainian nationalism is more muted than elsewhere in western Ukraine. The region's 200,000-strong Hungarian minority champion their own rights in Ukraine, and have a vocal ally in Hungary's Prime Minister Viktor Orban. [2]

Finally (as far as the western part of the country goes), the region of Chernivtsi. This Ukrainian-settled land was awarded to Romania in the Austro-Hungarian disintegration, with no attempt to secure popular assent, either from emigrants to the USA or anywhere else. In 1940 the USSR successfully demanded its transfer to Soviet Ukraine, at the same time as it also annexed Bessarabia from Romania. The bulk of this latter territory now constitutes Moldva, but southern Bessarabia (which had been ruled by Russia, not Austria pre-1914) today forms the western part of Ukraine's Odessa province. As in Transcarpathia, militant Ukrainian nationalism has less traction here than in Galicia.

The rest of Ukraine – the land in the centre of the country and to the south and east, together constituting the bulk of both population and territory – all formed part of the Tsarist Empire (divided among multiple provinces, with no central Ukrainian political expression) and then Soviet Ukraine. Here too, however, there is diversity. The area known as Donbas in the south-east of the country – broadly the present contested and heavily-industrial provinces of Luhansk and Donetsk, have always had a high ethnic Russian, as well as Russophone, population. They could just as easily have been placed in Soviet Russia as Soviet Ukraine when the two republics regulated their internal (within the USSR) frontier in the 1920s. It is possible that their allocation to the Ukraine was due to a desire by the Bolshevik Party to add some strong proletarian ballast to the otherwise largely-peasant Ukraine. Soviet Ukraine was governed from Kharkiv, in the more working-class and Russian east and presently in the thrall of a dictatorial Ukrainian nationalist administration, for its first decade before the republican capital was moved to Kiev in 1934. The term Novorossiya (New Russia), now revived by some Russian nationalists and very briefly by Putin himself, covers the eight provinces in the east and south of Ukraine (plus Crimea), up to Odessa in the west. The term is not a recent invention – it was used to define the territory administratively under the Tsars from the mid-18th century up until 1917. Its transfer to the Ukraine in 1922 was, writes Richard Sakwa "as controversial then as it has once again become now." The centre and north of the country, including Kiev, once a largely Russian city in a Ukrainian countryside, has largely lacked both the Russian orientation of the south and east and the visceral nationalism of much of the west. [3]

One territory has moved in the other direction – Transnistria. This strip of land now forms, from the legal point of view, the eastern part of Moldva, previously the Moldavian Soviet Republic. Most of Moldavia was constituted by the northern part of Bessarabia, annexed by the USSR from Romania in 1940 (the southern part joining Soviet Ukraine at the same time). Transnistria was transferred to the new soviet republic from Soviet Ukraine. It is therefore the only territory of pre-1940 Soviet Ukraine not now in the independent Ukraine. As with the Crimea, such niceties may have mattered little within the context of the USSR, but they of course have come to matter a great deal since – Transnistria's people have voted to unite with Russia (from which it is geographically separated by the breadth of Ukraine) and exit from Moldova, creating one of the so-called "frozen conflicts" in former Soviet territory. The main thing frozen in this and other cases is the right to self-determination, which nobody seems keen to extend to the peoples forming minorities within the ex-soviet republics.

So Ukraine today includes territories which were always (pre-1991) ruled from Moscow, either by the Tsars or the Communist Party, territories which were never so ruled before 1939 or even 1945, and those which were part of the Russian empire before the first world war but lost to it as one of the war's consequences, and then passed to Soviet control during the second world war. Those which were not part of Soviet Ukraine from its inception were variously included in Poland, Czechoslovakia, Hungary or Romania between the wars. A citizen born in the city of Uzhgorod before 1914 could by 1992 have lived in the Austro-Hungarian Empire, the western Ukrainian and then Ukrainian National republics briefly installed after world war one, Czechoslovakia, Hungary, the USSR and independent Ukraine, all without moving house. And these are not merely questions of political affiliation – they also reflect different experiences of discrimination and oppression, different historical possibilities for national and cultural expression and different class developments. It is true to say that before 1914 all Ukranians, conscious of themselves as that or not, were oppressed. But their oppressors were not all the same – Russians, Poles, Hungarians all had a share, as have Germans subsequently.

Ukraine 1991 therefore reflected political decisions made about its borders over a period of some 75 years. It included Russians who did not really want to be there, just as it excluded Ukrainians living in adjacent areas placed in the Russian Federation. Ukraine could just as easily have been somewhat larger or a good deal smaller than it is today. These are questions nationalists can argue over until the cows come home, but it is still the case that the frontiers of Ukraine bear a particularly arbitrary colouring, a fact which has no legal weight from the perspective of international jurisprudence, but a fairly profound one from a more popular point of view. When the Rukh independence movement sought to mobilise opinion in 1990 it organised a "human chain" of a million people forming a line from Lviv in the west to Kiev in the centre of the country. The line looked to go no further east – independence knew where its frontiers lay, and they were not the same as those of Ukraine itself. [4]

None of this should have meant that Ukraine was in some way doomed as an independent and united state from the start. The fissures of history and ethnicity briefly summarised here are not unusual, still less unique. They also afflict other sovereign states, and a path through them can be navigated, given flexibility and democratic good-will. In the Ukrainian context this would have meant a pluralistic approach to statehood, acknowledging diversity in language, culture and national orientation; a democratic political system which, at least to the extent normal in European capitalist states, promoted popular well-being and national development; and a recognition by all powers, primarily the USA and its NATO associates, that Ukraine was no suitable site for geopolitical games, as any attempt to draw it into bloc politics would clearly be a recipe for disaster. This, of course, is not what happened in any respect, with the first 24 years of independent Ukrainian statehood instead offering a harrowing study in authoritarian kleptocracy, base chauvinistic positioning and irresponsible self-interested meddling by external powers.

Wall Street Journal editorial writer Matthew Kaminski, a neo-conservative, unwittingly highlighted the problem, writing at the height of the 2014 crisis: "To speak of a Ukrainian nation has long been a cause for argument. At the turn of the last century, Ukrainian historians and polemicists offered competing visions. Vyacheslav Lypynsky's has won out. He said Ukraine needed a state first to create a nation…the Polish aristocrat Lypynsky said his Ukrainian nation shouldn't and couldn't be about ethnicity or language, but an idea. Ukraine got its state only in 1991, and inclusion is its national identity." Kaminsky could have added that with no idea beyond oligarchic pillage, and a dysfunctional state subordinated to that project and nothing else, the Ukrainian political culture has indeed defaulted onto the reliable stand-bys of nationalism - ethnicity and language - and as a consequence is anything but inclusive today. [5]

When?

So much for borders and sovereignties. The national question in 20th century Ukraine is entwined with the class question, and particularly with the seventy-year history of Soviet socialism in Ukraine and the rest of the USSR. This history has itself become a battlefield over which competing versions of contemporary Ukraine are fought.

The leading English-language historian of the Ukraine is blunt: "Ukrainian nationalism, in both the Russian and the Austrian Empire, belongs to the intelligentsia-inspired variety." He adds, saliently, that "people are not born with a national identity; they must learn that they belong to a particular nationality." The 19th century was the age of the manufacture of such identities, within and beyond all the great Empires of the age. Today, Ukrainians are being force-fed a national definition which many are deeply uncomfortable with. Down to the fall of Tsarism, it is broadly true to assert that Ukrainian national identity was overwhelmingly the preoccupation of the emerging, and thinly-spread intellectual and cultural elite in Russian-ruled Ukraine (socialists among them). The Ukrainian-speaking peasantry either held a Ukrainian identity alongside other points of association which they did not consider competitive, or they did not have such an identity at all. They shared their territory and their lives with ethnic Russians and Russified Ukrainians, amongst others. Religion and loyalty to the Tsar were as important as any sense of being Ukrainian. Most Ukrainians in the ex-Tsarist territories "were Orthodox peasants with as yet only a limited sense of broader identity" in the words of another historian. [6]

Sir John Maynard, one of the most eminent historians of the Tsarist Empire of the first half of the twentieth century, described Ukraine thus:

> "The line of demarcation between Great-Russia and Ukraine is difficult to draw. There is no clear division between the two in the north; there are foreign colonies in the south-west, sometimes called New Russia. The towns are almost entirely populated by non-Ukrainians or by Russified Ukrainians. The Donets basin is filled with workers from outside, many of them Asiatic in origin; Kharkov is alien in sprit to Ukraine. It has been estimated that not more than half of those shown in the statistics to be Ukrainians have any stable or convinced sense of nationality...except as the result of a ruinous foreign war...the acceptance by Russia of separation from Ukraine is unthinkable." [7]

These factors are not what sets Ukrainian nationalism apart, however. The emergence of national consciousness across the eastern half of Europe in the 19th century was everywhere the work of intellectuals, scattering seed on predominantly peasant soil. The distinctive feature in Ukraine was that the working-class scarcely even began to emerge in a national context – rather, it was a product of the Soviet years, founded upon a largely Russian emigrant basis, at least across what became Soviet Ukraine pre-1939. Unity with Russian workers (and those from other Soviet nationalities to some extent) was scarcely an idea externally imposed on the workers of Ukraine, but one inherent from the emergence of both Ukrainian nationalism and a Soviet project based on working-class internationalism. This class factor can hardly be discounted.

Nevertheless, as already noted, the Ukrainian idea gave birth to three separate short-lived republics between 1918 and 1921, statelets which made up for their considerable deficiency in mass support by the sponsorship of foreign powers. By 1922, however, the Ukrainian Socialist Soviet Republic was a constituent element of the USSR, and the rest of Ukrainian inhabited territories were under the control of new-born bourgeois states to the west, Poland above all. Soviet Ukraine's history became indivisible from that of the Soviet Union for the next seventy years.

That experience transformed Ukraine in ways which were not specific to it – educational and literacy levels soared, and the country's industry developed exponentially. People of different nationalities lived together well enough for the most part, united by a Soviet ideal or, when and where this faltered, at least cushioned by citizenship of a functioning state which delivered a very high level of social security. On the other hand, its political system ossified, its Communist cadre and other sections of the population suffered enormously during the purges of 1937-38, while the economy (and ultimately all of society with it) came to stagnate in the 1970s and 1980s although, as Andrew Wilson argues, "…after almost half a century of constant traumas since 1914 the peace and relative prosperity of the 1960s and 1970s were undoubtedly attractive to many Ukrainians." [8]

All of this, to one degree or another, affected all the peoples and republics of the USSR, and forms part of its common heritage. There are, however, three questions specific (or to be exact, more specific) to Ukraine which reverberate in contemporary politics and therefore need touching on here – the issue of cultural and national oppression in the Soviet Ukraine; the famine of the early 1930s, and whether this constituted an attempted "genocide" of Ukrainians by the Soviet power; and the Ukrainian experience during the second world war. In highlighting these questions, the greater salience of the larger, common, history, of a breakneck and comprehensive modernisation (perhaps the main post-war appeal of Communist Parties in those parts of Europe where they ruled) punctuated by astonishing achievements and calamities, should not be belittled or set aside. It has done as much to shape contemporary Ukrainian political identity as the more Ukraine-focussed agenda. However, it is the latter side of the total Ukrainian experience which is invoked to justify contemporary political postures, on the nationalist side above all.

National oppression?

The early years of Communist rule reflected the party's ideological commitment to class-based politics and, in that setting, to national equality in a multi-national socialist state, with the right to self-determination as a core principle. To that end, it opposed great-Russian chauvinism first of all, and worked to elevate the cultural level of peoples long-repressed by the Tsarist regime. This was not the challenge in the Ukraine that it was in parts of Central Asia, for example, but it was a challenge nevertheless. Class-based as it was, over two-thirds of the Bolshevik Party's membership in Ukraine was not ethnic Ukrainian in the year of Lenin's death, 1924 – this reflecting the fact that the republic's working class was concentrated in the Russian-populated Donbas, the mines and factories of which had absorbed tens of thousands of emigrants from the east during Tsarism's last years. Nevertheless a policy of "Ukrainisation" was followed fairly consistently up until the mid-1930s. This meant promoting Ukrainian culture, language and cadres within Soviet Ukraine. By 1933, sixty per cent of the party's membership there was ethnic Ukrainian, and 92 per cent of the newspaper circulation in the Republic was in the Ukrainian language. 97 per cent of primary school children in the republic were in Ukrainian-language schools by 1929. [9]

The climate started to change somewhat in the mid-1930s. Among the negative reasons was a growing anxiety that national differences could provide fissures along which the Soviet state could break up, an outlook which reached an obsessive and pathological pitch in the prophylactic "national operations" launched by the NKVD in 1937-38 and aimed at eradicating any popular base for national secessionism – dressed up as counter-espionage of course - within the union. More positively, there was a need to form a common culture, political unity and language of communication to cement the emerging Soviet state. Both perspectives militated in favour of tighter central control from Moscow and of elements of Russification, the more so in those republics like Ukraine where Russians and Ukrainians had closely inter-mingled over centuries, and ethnic Russians were a considerable portion of the population. Certainly, the idea that foreign powers would look to sever Ukraine from the USSR was not a paranoid fantasy of Stalin's – Hitler had set it down in black and white, and more limited Polish ambitions were also a matter of record – and the notion that nationalism might be the lever to do so was also logical. "We may lose Ukraine", Stalin wrote to his party deputy Lazar Kaganovich in 1932 at the height of the grain crisis, reflecting a constant preoccupation of the Soviet leadership. The "greatest danger" in Soviet nationalities policy, which in the 1920s had been Russian chauvinism, was now seen as nationalism, although the former was not entirely discounted as a problem. In November 1933 the Ukrainian Congress of Soviets wove the two themes together in a declaration that that "the greatest danger is now local Ukrainian nationalism since it has allied itself with international intervention [against the USSR]" [10]

This fed into a Russifying tendency, including in the sensitive matter of laungauge. Nikita Khruschev's speech to a Ukrainian party congress in 1938 is representative of the logic, mixing class and national formulae promiscuously:

"...all the people study the Russian language because...the Russian workers have set an example to the workers and peasants of the whole world....People of all areas are studying the Russian language in order to study Leninism and Stalinism....The bourgeois nationalists, the Polish and German spies, as they made their way into certain sections of the cultural front...drove the Russian language from schools. But the Ukrainian people, who in the course of many centuries have battled against their enemies alongside the Russian workers and peasants, are completely dedicated to the general aspirations of the working class of the Soviet world. They are tied by vital bonds to the Great Russian people..." [11]

Ukrainian language and culture remained protected, alongside Russian, throughout the Soviet years in Ukraine. Ethnic Ukrainians predominated in the Republic's leadership, and formed a powerful lobby within the CPSU and the USSR as a whole. Some, from Mikola Skrypnyk in the 1920s down to Pyotr Shelest in the 1960s and early 1970s represented a form of "national communism" aiming to articulate Ukrainian national aspirations within a Soviet framework – both were in the end dismissed by Moscow, but not before they had registered a profound influence. Furthermore, several leaders who played a large role on the all-Union stage – Khrushchev and Brezhnev among them- came from the Ukraine and/or had a mixed

Ukrainian heritage. Up to a point, ideas of Ukrainian nationhood were accommodated, as the idea of one merged Soviet people was supplanted by the more realistic position of a community of Soviet peoples, sometimes mixed with a pan-Slavism that had a certain post-war constituency too. In the last years of the USSR, a little under half of children in the Ukraine enrolled in Ukraine-language schools, and more than a quarter of books were published in the language – a decline from the 1930s, but arguably an understandable one in a society where almost all read Russian, and certainly not a state of cultural annihilation.

No case can be made for Ukraine having been exploited economically to the advantage of Russia. Instead, its industry and culture developed rapidly during the Soviet years. Nor did the Communist government try to make Ukrainians Russian. Instead it tried to make them Soviet, as it did the Russians themselves. This project may have had limited success in the former Polish and Austrian ruled territories in the west, but it certainly shaped the values of millions of Ukrainians. As Aleksander Bik, an ordinary citizen from the east of Ukraine, told a western reporter during the uprising in Donbas in 2014. "They call us traitors and separators. But I don't feel like a traitor. I felt like a traitor before, when I had to call myself Ukrainian. I don't feel like a traitor now." [12]

Magocsi sums up the result of the Soviet years thus: "…the twentieth century created in Soviet Ukraine a highly educated, bilingual, nationally conscious and largely urban population…" And Richard Sakwa likewise: "Throughout the vicissitudes of war, division and domination, the idea of Ukrainian nationhood was never extinguished, but it was balanced by commitment to the larger Soviet project, which brought with it industrialisation, urbanisation and the creation of a relatively modern and educated society." The idea that Ukraine was a nation oppressed by the USSR, while doubtless a view felt by many of those who lived in those parts of the country which had never formed part of the Tsarist Empire, nor been included in the USSR before the war, is hard to sustain. Scotland, perhaps, with real cultural and political grievances against an over-centralised regime, but not Ireland, held only by fire and sword for centuries. [13]

Genocide by Famine?

The collectivisation of Soviet agriculture was a trauma from which Soviet society arguably, and farm productivity undoubtedly, never fully recovered. Aimed at modernising agriculture at a pace which would allow for accelerated investment in industrial development in turn, while cementing the USSR's social base through the elimination of the rural bourgeois class, it was accompanied by high levels of violence and vast social disruption across the countryside.

That this also led to famine in Ukraine in 1931-32 has become one of the foundation stories of Ukrainian independence – the holodomor. The famine is far from being a fiction, but in its wilder dramatisations it has become history rendered unintelligible in the service of the nationalist political project: "the regime change of memory" in one historian's phrase. The idea that the famine was deliberately organised by the Soviet regime in order to break or destroy the Ukrainian nation, and that it led to ten million deaths, is energetically promoted by Ukrainian nationalists (who mainly hail from those parts of contemporary Ukraine not in the Soviet Union in the 1930s). Former President Yuschenko was particularly active in promoting this story, which serves obvious anti-Russian purposes. This presentation, aimed at hanging the "genocide" label around the Soviet Union's neck, did not in fact originate in the Ukraine at all, but in the USA and Canada in the 1980s, as Wemheuer shows, and was re-exported to Ukraine to become a primordial myth legitimising the new state when it found itself independent rather to its surprise and its nationalist protagonists sorely required definition against "the other". [14]

Serious researchers and demographers estimate that famine deaths in Ukraine would have been around 2.5 to three million – a horrifying enough figure, but a long way from the ten million favoured by Ukrainian nationalists and their present-day supporters on the far left. The real issue is whether this dreadful episode was consciously willed by the Soviet government for political objectives, or, in a more diluted form, whether the suffering was simply ignored in favour of higher state interests (feed the cities first; export of grain for hard currency) and a willingness to see a hostile peasantry decimated when famine started to take hold.

The idea that Stalin wished to destroy Ukraine as a nation is hard to take seriously. First, the Bolshevik government was animated by class, not national principles – its formidable powers of hatred were class-focussed. Throughout, Ukraine was regarded as a "Soviet nation", internally differentiated on class grounds but never suspect as a whole. The mass starvation in Ukraine flowed in part from political decisions affecting the USSR as a whole. Wilson's judgement that the famine "was an ideological not a national war" is to that extent correct. [15]

Secondly, the famine of the early 1930s also affected many Russian-populated areas, while Kazakhstan, where an attempt to settle a nomadic population allied to the socialisation of livestock led to disastrous consequences, was worst hit of all – it cannot be argued that Stalin's government wanted to destroy all the nations of the USSR. The present Russian authorities, confronting Ukraine's claims on this point, argue that collectivisation and its consequences was a common tragedy for the peoples of the USSR at the time. And for a leader with supposed genocidal intentions towards Ukrainians, Stalin seemed uncommonly fond of acquiring larger numbers of them – in 1939, 1940 and 1946 more and still more Ukrainian-populated territories were annexed to the USSR, as we have outlined. Ukraine was larger and stronger by the time Stalin died than ever before in its history.

Moreover, more recent research has shown that the Communist Party Politburo at the time did – haltingly, and too late for many – approve famine relief measures and authorise a reduction in state grain requisitions in Ukraine. Undoubtedly, it subordinated the requirements of humanitarianism to the goals of maintaining the development of the country's industrial and military capacity, which required feeding the cities first and maintaining trading relations with the encircling capitalists. And there can be no argument that for too long credible reports of immense suffering in the Ukrainian countryside were dismissed as the work of weak-minded activists at best, or counter-revolutionary propaganda at worst. No-one in the Moscow leadership of the time anticipated anything like the resistance to collectivisation, conceived as an essentially tool of modernisation, which eventuated; nor could conceive of it as anything other than counter-revolutionary in inspiration, irrespective of ethnicity.

Nevertheless, it appears that it was a famine blundered into, rather than engineered, that it was a product of centrally-driven policies, considerably exacerbated by poor weather, which affected many parts of the USSR without distinction as to nationality, and that once the calamity became incontrovertible, the government sought to mitigate it, however inadequately, including by mobilising the Communist Party in the Ukraine to assist the affected areas.

That is broadly the view of the historians who have studied the matter most closely, R.W. Davies and Stephen Wheatcroft above all. They estimate around 5 million deaths from hunger and famine-related disease in the USSR as a whole, including the calamity in Kazakhstan. Human losses in Ukraine may account for half of that awful figure. They attribute the famine, outside weather-related causes, to "the modus operandi of the Soviet system as it was established under Stalin. They were formulated by men with little formal education and limited knowledge of agriculture. Above all they were a consequence of the decision to industrialise this peasant country at breakneck speed." In a deeply hostile international environment, it might have been added. [16]

The main proponent of the alternative view - that the famine was deliberately willed by the Communist authorities for political purposes; the view now promulgated by the Ukrainian regime, was Robert Conquest, high priest of anti-Soviet history. Even he, however, according to Davies and Wheatcroft, finally conceded that it was not his view that "Stalin purposely inflicted the 1933 famine. No. What I argue is that with resulting famine imminent, he could have prevented it, but put 'Soviet interests' other than feeding the starving first…". Norman Naimark, assembling all the evidence he can to convict Stalin of genocide, also acknowledges that "there is not a lot of evidence that Stalin himself ordered the killer famine," although he knew about it. Naimark claims not that Stalin wanted to kill or deport all the Ukrainians but rather that he wished to transform Ukraine into a Soviet nation through brutal means, regarding the peasantry as "enemies of the people". Even this case he struggles to substantiate from sources rather than by assertion, but as far as it goes, it nevertheless undermines any assertion that these terrible events were targeted at the destruction of the Ukrainian people. [17]

In so far as the story of "Soviet genocide" against Ukraine is one of the myths that underpin aggressive Ukrainian nationalism today, with its anti-Russian focus, and the latter in turn legitimises the expansion of the institutions of world imperialism up to Russia's borders, then the effort to establish some sort of historical clarity on the dreadful questions of the 20th century serves the interests of peace in the 21st.

World War in Ukraine

The last time Ukraine was thus fought over was during World War Two. The bald sequence of events was this – Germany declared war on Poland, its aggression swiftly overwhelming the Polish state. Acting under secret understandings reached with the Nazis ancillary to the Non-Aggression Treaty signed the previous month, the Red Army then moved into Poland from the east, taking control of the mainly Ukrainian and Belarussian majority areas to the east of the Curzon line, land which Pilsudski had seized in 1921. These areas were then annexed to their respective Soviet republics, as were the former Romanian territories mentioned above in 1940. In 1941, when Hitler invaded the USSR not only these western regions but the entirety of the Ukraine (and of course more besides) fell under the control of the Nazis (or their Romanian allies in respect of small territories), and were subjected to intense colonial oppression and exploitation with the collaboration of nationalists, including the extermination of their Jewish population and many more besides. As the Red Army moved to liberate

Ukraine from the end of 1943 onwards, a bloody four-cornered struggle developed – between the Soviet Army and the Nazis over the whole of Ukraine, with Ukrainian nationalists (ONU-UPA) fighting alongside the Nazis for the most part in the hope of establishing some form of Ukrainian puppet state west of the Dnieper, and Polish underground forces seeking to retrieve the Pilsudski territories for a reconstituted greater Poland. In the end, of course, Soviet rule was restored over all of 1941 Ukraine, to which Transcarpathian Ukraine was then added.

This brief summary encompasses a world of death and suffering of course. Academician Yuri Kondufor of the Ukrainian Academy of Sciences gave the first comprehensive Soviet estimate of Ukrainian wartime deaths in 1984. He stated that there was a total loss of 7.5 million (7,509,045) people including the dead and those taken as slave labour to Germany. The war and German occupation resulted in the death 3,898,457 civilians in Ukraine and 1,366,588 military and prisoners-of-war. In addition 2,244,000 Ukrainian citizens were taken to Germany for slave labour in war industries, few of whom returned alive. To this could be added the loss of 250,159 people in Transcarpathian Ukraine and Crimea (neither of them part of Soviet Ukraine at the time) giving a total of 7,759,204 deaths. [18]

These figures include about 600,000 Ukrainian Jews, mainly victims of the Nazi genocide, but also slaughtered by the ONU and, to a lesser extent, Polish forces in western Ukraine in the course of the war. Of all the competing military forces which ranged across Ukraine's territory in those terrible years only the Red Army did not have among its aims the eradication of Ukraine's huge Jewish population. No section of the Soviet people suffered more.

The collective suffering has not yielded a common narrative regarding the war. Ukrainians did not all fight on the same side, although the divisions were not of equal substance. About 90,000 served in the nationalist and collaborationist ONU, fighting alongside the Nazis; while at least 2.5 million enlisted in the Red Army, of whom the most eminent was perhaps Marshal Andrey Yeremekno, commander of the Soviet forces at Stalingrad, one of the pivotal events on which world history has turned.

The war came to Ukrainian territory in September 1939 with the occupation and subsequent annexation of the eastern provinces of Versailles Poland. Only those which were annexed to Soviet Ukraine concern us here, but other areas were joined to Soviet Belorussia, including the Bialystok region, which was included in the Soviet Union only until 1944, when it was restored to the re-emerging Poland; thereby constituting the only territory to ever be included within the USSR and then subsequently excluded again by Moscow's own volition. It should also be noted that it was as a result of the Soviet occupation that then still-independent Lithuania gained the Polish province of Wilnow (now Vilnius), gifted them by Moscow. Some Lithuanians today do not like being reminded of the fact that they owe the possession of their capital to Molotov's diplomacy, and that their state was the third beneficiary of the provoked collapse of Poland in 1939. The irony of Lithuanian nationalists simultaneously campaigning for independence from the USSR on their Soviet boundaries and for a denunciation of the Molotov-Ribbentrop Pact in 1939 was widely noted at the time.

The Red Army moved into eastern Poland under the banner of revolution. "The general ideological framework of the Red Army's assignment – class and national liberation – was certainly known to all" in the newly-occupied areas, according to one unsympathetic writer. [19]

The area was both ready and unready for such a transformation. The majority Ukrainian population had been second-class citizens in inter-war Poland, discriminated against and subject to the rule of Polish gentry. Eastern Poland was among the most backward areas of

Europe, with the vast majority of the population subsisting in an impoverished and undeveloped countryside, lacking almost all amenities or opportunities for cultural improvement. To that extent, much of the population was ready to embrace emancipation from Polish domination, and ripe for the sort of accelerated economic and social transformation which Soviet power had wrought further east. Yet the working-class, where Communism sought its natural social base, was tiny in western Ukraine, and the local Communist party correspondingly small. Nor did Ukrainians who desired freedom from Warsaw necessarily welcome governance from Moscow.

Nevertheless, even hostile historians acknowledge that the Red Army received an initial warm response from the population, amidst this slew of contradictory impulses. Jan Gross writes: "For the record it must be stated unambiguously: throughout the Western Ukraine and Western Belorussia, in hamlets, villages and towns, the Red Army was welcomed by smaller or larger but, in any case, visible, friendly crowds. These were largely composed of young people from the so-called ethnic minorities – Belorussians, Jews and Ukrainians". These minorities, of course, aggregated to a considerable majority in these areas. Communist songs were sung along with religious hymns. "Entering troops were sometimes showered with flowers, embraced and kissed..." [20]

Gross writes further: "The overwhelming majority of the Ukrainians were sincerely glad to see the collapse of the Polish state, and this is what they were celebrating when they cheered the Red Army....great excitement circulated among Ukrainians because an intolerable situation of ethnic discrimination had finally come to an end." [21]

Of course, the situation speedily became more complicated. For one thing, the expectation among Red Army officers that their arrival would stimulate a mass revolutionary uprising among the oppressed was confounded, and their efforts to stimulate class warfare in the newly-Soviet areas generally foundered on local indifference. Social transformations to align western Ukraine with the Soviet system were therefore engineered from above, with the customary imprisonments, deportations and other depredations associated with the NKVD, alongside an expansion of schools, universities and cultural outlets and a considerable development of industrial and agricultural production. The second problem, and by far the greater one over the longer-term was that while the huge Jewish population of the area almost universally preferred Soviet to German rule for obvious reasons (sometimes somewhat vitiated by concerns over Bolshevik intentions towards private property); the ethnic Ukrainians were more ambivalent. Some saw German rule as preferable – once the despised Poles had been seen off – since it might permit the creation of a Ukrainian puppet state in due course. This was, broadly, the position of Stepan Bandera and his Ukrainian National Organisation (OUN).

Bandera is now celebrated as a national hero across many parts of Ukraine, and in the west of the country especially. Ukrainian nationalism exalts his person and his cause, and its more extreme elements see merit in his methods too. The OUN had been founded in 1929 as an underground organisation to promote a Ukrainian state. It mainly worked in the Polish-ruled Ukraine before the war, but Soviet Ukraine was not entirely neglected. Bandera became leader of its more militant wing, committed to terrorism.

Bandera's OUN was violently anti-Semitic, as well as anti-Russian, anti-Soviet and anti-Polish. The German SS recorded in July 1941 that the group's slogan was "Long live Ukraine without Jews, Poles and Germans; Poles behind the river San, Germans to Berlin, and Jews to the gallows".

In June 1941, Bandera's forces raced to Lviv in the wake of the Nazi vanguard to proclaim the Ukrainian puppet state which they earnestly hoped Hitler would permit. On arrival it declared a "revived Ukrainian state [which] will cooperate closely with Nazi Great Germany...the Ukrainian National Revolutionary Army, to be formed on Ukrainian soil, will henceforth fight along with the allied German Army against Muscovite occupation for a sovereign United Ukrainian State and a new order in the whole world." [22]

Alas for Bandera, he had underestimated the depths of German racial contempt for the Slavs. He was neither the first nor the last to learn that Hitler was exclusively a German nationalist (imperialist, in fact) and not a benign patron of all nationalisms in Europe. An independent Ukraine formed no part of his plans – rather, the Ukrainians were to be worked to death as colonial slave labour for the Reich, and their land eventually populated by German settlers. Eric Koch, appointed Reich Commissar for the Ukraine, summed up the regime's attitude bluntly: "The attitude of the Germans must be governed by the fact that we deal with a people that is inferior in every respect....There must be no sentimentality. This people must be governed by us by iron force, so as to help us win the war now. We have not liberated it to bring blessings on Ukraine but to secure for Germany the necessary living space and a source of food." [23]

Under these circumstances, Bandera's forces concentrated on infiltrating the police and other institutions left in place in Ukraine. While the OUN did occasionally engage German forces, the only significant underground resistance in Ukraine was supplied by the Soviet partisans. Bandera's focus remained on opposing the Soviet forces, killing Jews and Poles and trying to inveigle Nazi Germany into some form of alliance. This policy bore fruit in 1944 when the retreating Germans declared in favour of an explicit alliance with Bandera who they accommodated in Berlin and funded lavishly. However, by this time the invaders had lost control of most of Ukraine to the advancing Red Army in any case, so there was no possibility of a Bandera-led state emerging. Bandera's troops thereafter fought alongside the Germans, while finding time and resources to kill around 130,000 Poles in western Ukraine, mostly women and children, in a pioneer exercise in ethnic cleansing.

Thereafter Bandera maintained a campaign of armed resistance to the restoration of Soviet rule in western Ukraine which lasted until the early 1950s. The duration of his campaign owed less to popular support (of which there was some, however) than to backing by the CIA, which took over this amongst other Nazi assets in the early days of the Cold War. Bandera himself was killed in Munich in 1959 by an agent of Soviet state security; and it is impossible to say that he deserved any different. He remains, however, an iconic figure in Ukrainian nationalist circles.

The experience of the Nazi occupation of Ukraine profoundly reinforced the base of Soviet power in Ukraine, including among sections of the population initially anti-Bolshevik or at any rate apathetic. This was due to its bestial character which was expressed first of all in anti-semitism, targeting Ukraine's Jewish population for the cruellest treatment and harshest repression, even before the move to organised genocide. Those sections of the population influenced by the Communist Party or Soviet power more generally opposed this persecution, while those in thrall to nationalism assisted it for the most part. [24]

The overall character of the occupation regime can be understood from Eric Koch's attitude quoted above. Material devastation was added to mass murder, and even such support as the invaders had found in western Ukraine at the outset tended to evaporate as the war continued, without ever disappearing entirely. Certainly the possibility, which some Nazi leaders had set great store by, of winning Ukrainian support on the basis of a national and anti-collectivisation programme, was squandered by Koch's racist brutality. "…Never before in the history of Ukraine did so many social and ethnic groups suffer so much during one period. Almost everyone experienced seemingly ceaseless humiliation, most notably abuse, and lived under a cloud of danger," writes historian Karel Berkhoff who, while forthright in his condemnation of Soviet abuses, rejects any idea of equivalent malevolence between Hitler and Stalin. [25]

Unsurprisingly then, one of the strongest anti-Nazi partisan movements of the entire war was created in Soviet Ukraine. The existence of this movement, distinct from if obviously closely allied with the Red Army and Soviet power structures more generally, also forms part of the legacy of the war in contemporary Ukraine. Partisans fought in their tens of thousands against not just the Nazis, but also Stepan Bandera and his OUN. It is scarcely surprising that when a movement venerating Bandera seized power in 2014, it ran into trouble.

Opposition to Nazi rule took many forms. After the Germans occupied the big industrial city of Kharkov in the east of Ukraine (its pre-1934 capital) they were unable to restart a single factory for three months because of worker resistance. Partisan resistance began almost immediately – the first attacks on German occupiers in Dnipropetrovsk was in October 1941 – but really mushroomed into a major fighting force in 1943, as the Red Army began to advance from Stalingrad. Partisan units often comprised thousands of fighters, as large as regular military formations, and established effective control over large areas behind the German front lines. According to recent research, workers or peasants made up 83 per cent of this force. [26]

Some of the complexities of the war years, which echo down to this day, are expressed in the remarkable book *The Underground Committee Carries On*, written by Ukrainian partisan commander Alexei Fyodorov. Before and after the war Fyodorov was a regional party official in Chernigov, to the north-east of Kiev, and elsewhere. During the conflict he was one of the major partisan leaders in occupied Ukraine, for which he was twice made a Hero of the Soviet Union. His book, published in the USSR in 1952, while Stalin was still very much among the living, is notable for its relative lack of paeans to the Soviet leader, and for its acknowledgement of the presence of Ukrainian nationalists and other anti-Soviet people among the population. There is no attempt to pretend that the partisans were swimming in 100 per cent friendly waters, or that the invaders found no local collaborators. Nevertheless, this book could only be published in Ukraine today at the risk of breaking the law, since its narrative is not that of the uber-nationalists in power. [27]

A pan-Soviet outlook was only strengthened by the course and outcome of the "Great Patriotic War". Some historians have argued that Red Army veterans in the Ukraine helped nurture a post-war "consciousness that was both Ukrainian and Soviet." That consciousness remains a live factor in Ukraine today, confounding any pro-Ukraine/pro-Russia over-simplifications. If the so-called holodomor has become the cornerstone of Ukrainian nationalist identity, the Great Patriotic War remains the emblem of Soviet unionism. [28]

Attempts to challenge it by the contemporary Kiev authorities may turn a trick in some parts of the country, but in others it is only a formula for exacerbating divisions. Take for example the Kiev-appointed Governor of Kherson province, who observed Victory Day (May 9) 2014 by making a pro-Hitler speech to a public rally. Since his audience was largely composed of people who had fought against Hitler (or their descendants), this was a sign of either incredible stupidity, or a malicious intention to provoke. Much of the audience booed and protested on what was supposed to be a day of united memory; a suitable raspberry blown at the Maidan movement's own imagined version of "Ukraine", a version which, as more recent events have shown, can only be inculcated by placing the full force of law behind it.

Which?

The attempt to force Ukraine and Ukrainians into a binary model – east/west, nationalist/Russian-oriented - is doubtless tempting for western pundits conditioned to see the world in gladiatorial terms, but it is unrealistic. A 1996 opinion poll found that 34% of the population of Ukraine identified primarily with Ukraine itself (mainly in the west), 3% with Russia, 17% with the USSR – and 37% with their own neighbourhood. [29]

That is not a surprising result. In March 1991, 82% of Ukrainian voters, on an 84% turnout, supported the retention of a federal union with Russia and most of the other Soviet republics. In December of the same year, 92% of voters, on a 94% turnout, supported Ukraine's declaration of independence. Furthermore, every election held in Ukraine since indicates that there is no stable majority either for a nationalist perspective or for a unionist (with Russia) one. EU membership, with its apparent offer of stability and prosperity (chimerical, as the Greeks and Spanish amongst others can testify) may well command majority assent, but then so too may erstwhile Soviet ideals of the "brotherhood of the peoples".

Nor, then, is it surprising that actual power in independent Ukraine has been held throughout by a "third force" – corrupt and competing clans of oligarchs who, having seized hold of the country's wealth and resources through a process of post-Soviet plunder, showed far less interest in developing a democratic culture, or indeed advancing any ideas whatsoever, than in rent-seeking and embedding their own particular interests in the interstices of the new state, playing on one popular prejudice or another to maintain a constituency of support for their rule. In the words of the inveterate anti-Russian journalist Timothy Garton Ash "there is a breath-taking scale of corruption and oligarchic misrule, which has deformed the state ever since it gained formal independence nearly a quarter of a century ago." [30]

Or, as *The Economist* reported:

> "Weak institutions, low morale and an underdeveloped sense of public service have made everyone from judges to traffic police liable to corruption over Ukraine's entire post-Soviet history. Murky privatisations...in the mid-1990s created a class of oligarchs who came to exercise outsized influence on politics and business. That the two main candidates for the presidency in the recent election – Petro Poroshenko and Yulia Tymoshenko – both made large fortunes through opaque deal-making in the 1990s shows the unshakeable dominance of the power structure formed in that era." [31]

The oligarchs have divided into clans based around places or people – Donbas, Dnipropetrovsk, Tymoshenko etc – and have sometimes competed but generally regulated their differences sufficiently to keep their mutual power intact. Together, 100 people control 80-85% of the country's wealth, Richard Sakwa estimates. (Sakwa, p61).

Parliamentary deputies, whatever party label they worse, were above all beholden to sponsoring oligarchs in most cases. The corruption and looting of state resources seems to have reached epic proportions under Yanukovych – even Vladimir Putin has publicly acknowledged this – but his nationalist predecessors were far from innocent. Yulia Tymoshenko's self-interested manipulation of the energy sector was also legendary. Indeed, Tymoshenko has been indicted for corruption and money-laundering in the USA, but mysteriously never prosecuted, although her co-conspirator, another former Prime Minister Pavel Lazarenko, was sentenced to eight years. [32]

This melange has barely constituted a ruling class in any conventional sense – a class with its own organics roots in society, its own organisations and culture, institutions for mediating internal differences, a definite policy towards other classes etc. Rather it is an agglomeration of gangs and clans, some rooted in former Soviet officialdom, others not, who moved swiftly to seize state assets (energy resources, factories etc) in a post-Soviet privatisation process which even some of their own number now acknowledge to have been corrupt, and have then built gaudy palaces for themselves and shipped billions abroad.

This elite has proved incapable of either coming to terms with Ukraine's past or fashioning a future for the country. There is no narrative beyond self-interest, and no hope for change on offer, from any of the squabbling factions. Since 1991 it has twisted this way and that, reflecting the divisions among the people yet uniting to maintain their own rent-seeking power. Even in western Ukraine, the state is regarded as "corrupt to its core" by many, according to *Le Monde Diplomatique*. The newspaper quotes a businessman who, accompanied as a matter of course by his private militia, told the local prosecutor in Khmelnytskyi that "for now you can talk to businessmen like us but soon, if this goes on, you'll have a proletarian revolution." East and west, same spectre, as we shall see. [33]

Ukraine's oligarchs are not very different in essence to their Russian compatriots. However, Ukraine has never undergone a "Putin process" whereby the state is strengthened (with significant authoritarian and anti-democratic limitations) sufficiently to at least circumscribe oligarchic power, in the political sphere particularly, and consolidate the robber elite into some form of ruling class with a story to tell and a social project to offer, however limited or even reactionary. Oil prices have doubtless helped. In Ukraine, the robbers have just been allowed to carry on robbing, utilising the balancing and manipulation, at least before 2014, of competing attitudes and identities among the people.

The consequences of oligarchic power have been catastrophic. Ukraine, despite its immense natural and industrial wealth (and a relatively liberal human rights regime), shares with Kyrgyzstan the distinction of being the only ex-Soviet republics where the economy is no larger than in 1991, when the USSR broke up. In its first decade of independence, the economy declined by a full sixty per cent! By comparison, neighbouring Belarus and Poland, not to mention Russia itself, have raced ahead. The country's population has plummeted by nearly twenty per cent, largely because of emigration, and a third of those who remain live below the poverty line. Unemployment stood at nearly ten per cent even before the Maidan crisis, and inflation at 20 per cent. [34]

Maidan Ukraine

The Maidan explosion was ignited by the (elected) government's decision not to proceed with the signing of an Association Agreement with the EU, in preference to an economic agreement with Russia. It would seem that this choice was made reluctantly, since the oligarchy would rather have not had to choose one way or another at all. The demonstrations in Kiev were also, however, demanding an end to corruption and broader democratic reforms, at least initially. Post-Maidan, little has changed for the better in Kiev. The government of Petro Poroshenko, a chocolate monopolist, has rested on two internal pillars – the nationalistic far right for muscle and order, and the oligarchs for governance. Externally, it has relied entirely on the patronage of the USA and other powers.

From the beginning, "Maidan" meant in practice the exchange of one set of oligarchs for another. Russian social democrat Boris Kagarlitsky wrote that "the class nature of the new regime in Kiev was demonstrated with striking clarity when billionaire oligarchs were appointed to key positions in the eastern regions. In exchange for 'stabilisation' they were offered the chance to privatise not only the economy in the eastern provinces, but also the functions of power." [35]

Yulia Tymoshenko herself was and is scarcely less a creature of the oligarchy than Yanukovych was. As the *Wall Street Journal* reported in March 2014 "at her prodding, the authorities in Kiev had appointed prominent business oligarchs to run the governments in Kharkiv, Donetsk and Dnepropetrovsk...these men won't please the pro-western activists who want a clear start for Ukrainian politics. Ms Tymoshenko's aides insist that reliable people are needed who can be counted on to bring these regions under control by the old methods of patronage politics and favours for business." Most of these appointees benefitted from crooked privatisations ordered by Tymoshenko when she was Prime Minister. While acknowledging that many privatisations in the Ukraine have been legally suspect, the US-installed Premier Arseniy Yatseniuk was swift to reassure one and all that "nationalisation is off the agenda". [36]

The newly-installed Governor of Donetsk, steel magnate Serhiy Taruta, began his first address to the people of the city he was appointed to head with the words "Dear Citizens, I address you as the Chairman of the Board of Directors of the Industrial Union of Donbas," which at least made his priorities clear. And a Professor at Donetsk University has said that "...the forces of SCM might be used to keep order". SCM is not a security service, but the name of the company System Capital Management, owned by Rinat Akhmetov, the 47th richest man in the world and described by a US Ambassador to Ukraine as "godfather" or the Donetsk business mafia, whose switch from supporting Yanukovych to the "Maidan" forces was decisive, not least for the group of Party of Regions MPs he effectively controls. [37]

The mandate of the new government of oligarchs was to slash state spending rapidly agreed by the post-Yanukovych Rada. Indeed, the *New York Times* reported in February 2014 that "among the reasons Mr Yanukovych turned away from signing political and trade accords with Europe in November was his unwillingness to carry our painful austerity measures and other reforms that had been demanded by the IMF." No such obstacles obstruct the neo-liberals in Kiev now. [38]

Poroshenko's own mandate is hardly robust – he and Tymoshenko between them secured fewer votes in the 2014 presidential elections than Yanukovych did on his own in 2010. And even the *Economist* wearily admitted that the parliamentary elections held in October 2014 "will not overhaul the system where deputies are extensions of business interests and can be sold and traded. The new parliament is likely to be dominated by old faces wearing new masks." [39]

The post-Maidan economic situation for ordinary people has been catastrophic. Heating costs have risen by around 40%, with domestic gas prices set to rise still further and older people now pay a tax of 15% on their pensions. Other welfare payments have been cut. The economy probably shrunk by around 7% in 2014, with farm production down by a third; and the collapse has only accelerated since, with the country looking at perhaps as much as 15% GDP reduction. Inflation is rising rapidly (over 60% in summer 2015), and unemployment is also increasing with as many as 120,000 civil servants facing lay-offs. Overall state spending is down by 17 per cent, and while authorities claim that the social welfare budget will rise by 30%, that is only half the rate of inflation, meaning a real-terms cut. The civil war in the east has dislocated the Kiev government from control of about a fifth of the national economy, including most of the coal mines. Foreign debt is a crippling and unsustainable debt 100% of GDP. [40]

Neo-liberalism does not, of course, intend to let this crisis go to waste. It provides the opening for a full-on take-over of the country by western imperialism, mediated through its familiar institutions of the EU and the IMF. There are forces within Ukraine, aided by the European Union above all, which will be pushing the country in a different direction – towards a transparent energy policy, reduced corruption, deregulation and a renewed banking system, shorn of its ties to the oligarchy. In a nutshell, this perspective aims at making of Ukraine a normal capitalist country. The problem is that the price for this transition will be overwhelmingly paid by ordinary people through higher unemployment and soaring prices for essentials, while it can be taken for granted that the wealth of the oligarchy will be protected, even if their political authority is eroded.

Poroshenko's surprise dismissal of Igor Kolomoisky, leading energy and banking sector oligarch (and like many such, a media tycoon to boot), as governor of Dnipropetrovsk in March 2015, ostensibly because of his abuse of his own private army to overtly advance his business interests, points in the direction of "normal capitalism". However, Kolomoisky was thanked for his efforts and sent on his way with his fortune intact – only his political office was taken from him. IMF-friendly commentators have praised Ukraine for at long last embarking on a "de-oligarchisation" process. However, if the age of oligarchs does start to fade it will be in favour of an austerity-driven neoliberal agenda from Brussels, backed by an authoritarian state sanctified in its repression by the nationalist discourse, the fears of proletarian revolution animating the business class of Lviv notwithstanding.

The irony is that this transition to a non-oligarchic capitalism, as preferred by the IMF, relies on the importation of foreign neo-liberals for its execution. Apparently the local material to hand was inadequate for the task. The appointment of former Georgian president Mikhail Saakashvili – he was voted out of office after launching the disastrous war against Russia in 2008. The city is the site of a massacre of an official 48 people by rampaging nationalists in 2014, although the real figure is much higher. The crime has not been investigated, something which has even drawn a rebuke from US Ambassador to the United Nations Samantha Power. Saakashvili's appointment to this key job by Poroshenko was surely intended as an insult to Russia and most of the local population alike, who may only tolerate their new chief because of Soviet-era memories of the time when Ukraine and Georgia were, after all, part of one country.

Other imports loom large in the Kiev power structure. The country's Finance Minister, Natalie Jaresko, is not only US-born but was also a State Department official for many years. Economy Minister Aivaras Abromavicius hails from Lithuania and has lived in the USA. Two other Georgian officials of the Saakashvili era serve as Health Minister and Deputy Prosecutor-General, while two more are Deputy Interior Ministers. The anti-Russian, pro-NATO caravan, having lost ground in Georgia, has simply decamped to Ukraine. The problem is hardly their nationality per se but the likelihood that they are simply in post to secure a project – the imposition of a "normal" neo-liberal capitalism in Ukraine, answering not to the people of the country but to the international institutions of the global capitalist order – before moving on once more. President Poroshenko has boasted in the *Wall Street Journal* that "alongside our ministers are many young people who have come to us from leading foreign and domestic companies...to join in our battle to overhaul our country." At any event, when Ms Jaresko has finished implementing her agenda – fuel price rises, tax cuts for business, big spending reductions on education and health, and the rest of the usual IMF austerity programme – she will most likely not be found in Ukraine. Nor will the collaboration of the IMF neo-liberals with the nationalist far-right be an enduring one, once it is determined who is the tiger and whom the rider. [41]

No less a dignitary of the Davos elite than Lawrence Summers, former US Treasury Secretary under Clinton, Economic Council Director under Obama, Harvard University President and all-round global deregulator and privatiser, has bestowed his blessing on the team in Ukraine. His argument also indicates that, when the chips are down, the strategic interests of the US world order can trump considerations of debt repayment, the considerations beggaring less strategically-vital debtors elsewhere in the world. Summers wrote in the *Financial Times*:

"The case for debt reduction [for Ukraine] is a strong as any I have encountered over the past quarter century. How the issue is resolved will say much about the extent of international commitment to Ukraine and resisting Russian aggression." Note the category shift, from failure to repay debt, usually a no-no in Summers' world, to standing up to Putin. No praise is too high for the economic junta in Kiev: "...Ukraine has its most reform-minded economic team since independence in 1991. It has shown real courage in...moving aggressively to curb energy subsidies that generated vast waste. The moral, geopolitical and economic case for the provision of strong support is compelling," he adds, in a revealing order of priorities. And since it has become clear that the Ukrainian government will be afforded a degree of latitude not offered to, say, the Greek. A large-scale debt write-down is in the offing, with a the senior US Treasury official responsible for international affairs telling creditors that such a deal would advance both their own interests and "Ukraine's economic and geopolitical fortunes." [42]

Another *Financial Times* columnist praised the new government as "...a fully paid-up member of the EU's policy consensus whereby all economic bliss comes from structural reforms". Within weeks of Yanukovych's flight, the Rada had passed fourteen bills of economic deregulation. A quick study of the blissed-out continent today shows where that leads, but comments like this indicate clearly who the Poroshenko-Yatseniuk team are working for. [43]

Unfortunately, however, they are losing the support of the people they are supposed to represent. The number of people who, according to opinion polling, have a positive view of the Poroshenko government has declined from 48 to 33 per cent over the last year. Even in western Ukraine, the number having a negative view of the Kiev regime has risen to over 50%, while Poroshenko has approval ratings of 22% for his handling of the economy. In a presidential election today, polling shows that Poroshenko would get just 14.6% of the vote, while premier Yatseniuk, the darling of the US State Department, would secure all of 1.3 per cent! [44]

Under these circumstances, it is not surprising that the transition to a neo-liberal economy is being supervised by a political regime which, if not fascist, is not exactly democratic either. The elected presidency of Yanukovich was overturned by force majeure, a combination of the street protests, increasingly led by the far right, and pressure from the western powers, primarily the USA. The elected parliament effectively crumbled thereafter. Both the new President, Poroshenko, and the new Rada (parliament) have also been elected. However, that is by no means the end of the story. Several factors and developments substantially vitiate the idea the Ukraine is now being run along democratic lines.

First, far right groups like Svoboda and Right Sector, while polling insignificantly in the elections, have entrenched their cadre deep in the reconfigured state apparatus, particularly in the security forces. Their fighters have been in the front line of waging the brutal war against the civilian population in the Donbas. Thousands of fascists have been armed and trained by the new regime to act as its spearhead against any and all forces resisting the new national narrative. Right Sector, in particular, is now an extremely well-armed and organised force, presently both leading the assault in the East and manoeuvring in the west to supplant Poroshenko. It and other groups are accreting strength as the state is seen to remain deeply dysfunctional and are increasingly staging provocations against the official Kiev authorities. Their popularity will likely rise as that of Poroshenko and his team falls.

Second, the Ukrainian Communist party has been effectively banned on Kiev-controlled territory, its offices attacked and its officials hounded; a prohibition which some on the nationalist right wish to extend to all political forces opposed to the new regime. For example, the Ivanovo-Frankivsk Regional Council has voted to ban all "anti-Ukrainian" parties, including those still represented in the Rada. Repressive action has also been taken against trade unions and other forces aligned with the movement in the Donbas. [45]

Third, the rule of law has substantially broken down. As noted, the new authorities have stalled any serious inquiry into the massacre at Odessa, or the shootings in Maidan Square at the climax of the movement to overthrow Yanukovych, shootings which many believe were not all (or not at all) the responsibility of the militia. In some parts of the country with more pro-Russian traditions, like Kharkov, a near reign of terror has been installed, with political prisoners being detained indefinitely without trial.

In this respect, particular mention should be made of the spate of "suicides" of former supporters of ex-President Yanukovych – at least eight in the first quarter of 2015. Many of these were clearly not suicides at all. Former state prosecutor Sergei Melnychuk, for example, was badly beaten before being apparently flung to his death in Odessa. Seven other Party of the Regions officials have also been found dead under mysterious circumstances. Media inquiries are met with the statement that all information about the deaths are state secrets, although four of the deaths have now been reclassified as murders. Whether the new regime is directly involved in the killings or not, or is merely covering up the enterprise of private individuals, it does not speak well for Ukraine's governance. [46]

Finally, there is the notorious law banning not only any display of symbols associated with the USSR but any characterisation of it as other than criminal; this a reference to a state which millions of Ukrainians lived under peaceably and sometimes proudly for their whole lives, and which millions more fought and died for. The same law exalts the Nazi collaborators as heroes of Ukraine's nationhood and, despite their record of mass murder and anti-semitic and anti-Polish as well anti-Soviet brutality, makes criticising them another crime. Even the 1918 Hetmanate, entirely a German creation, is given legal protection, a point at which the official effort to create a Ukrainian national narrative by decree reaches absurdity. Needless to say, this excess of triumphalist nationalism can only further polarise and divide Ukraine's people and can only be enforced through further repression. Singing the old Soviet national anthem can get you five years in prison.

To set against this dystopia, there is the possibility, however slim, of a more conventionally democratic Ukraine emerging from the crisis, with all its cross-currents. On the one hand, some observers at least believe that the earliest days of the Maidan movement included a democratic impulse. Kiev sociologist Volodymyr Ishchenko, for example, told the *New Left Review* that liberals and progressives were significant in the first days of Maidan and, had they not succumbed to the far right and the nationalist extremists, "they could have put forward something like a bourgeois-democratic agenda – for strong civil rights, no police abuse, against corruption and so on – which eastern Ukrainians could easily have supported too." Their sense of their own weakness, Ishchenko argues, led them to increasingly rely on the fascist right. The regime of Poroshenko, dependent on IMF-ordered neo-liberals, somewhat tamed oligarchs and neo-fascist volunteer battalions as it is, is clearly no harbinger of such an enlightened bourgeois-democratic agenda, for all that some sections of Ukrainian society will continue to sincerely push for it. While the Kiev government is bleeding popularity and credibility, there is as yet no serious development of a "third force" to counter the nationalist right on the one hand and the neo-liberal supporters of capitalism on the other. [47]

"People's Republican" Ukraine

On the other side of the country is the more profound social movement in the Donbas, inspired above all by fear as to what unalloyed nationalist domination in Kiev, allied to a savage EU austerity agenda, would mean for their own regions, culture and traditions. A far more industrialised region than western Ukraine, with still potent heavy industry and coal mining, the traditional identity of the Donbas is more class-oriented than nationalist. It is wrong to reduce the anti-Kiev movement in the eastern regions to manipulation from Moscow, although it cannot be doubted that the latter has played its part. The insurgency has its own origins, demands and aspirations, and they are not necessarily Putinesque.

Boris Kagarlitsky, in an autumn 2014 interview, portrayed the uprising which led to the creation of "People's Republics" in Donetsk and Luhansk, covering large parts of the two provinces including their major cities, in sweeping terms: "What is happening in Novorossiya is a revolutionary movement, though it's not yet a revolution in terms of social change....nowhere for so many years – perhaps since the Spanish revolution – have we see thousands of workers, or even hundreds of thousands, mobilised.

"There are thousands of workers in arms. And of course the Moscow oligarchs are scared of it spreading into Russia. Quite a lot of people speak about socialism. Others speak of a compromised version of a social republic, which means a welfare state, social priorities and some socialisation of property, including factories, mines and railways. The current leadership of Donetsk republic was reluctant to implement even those changes...It's quite normal that you have a bourgeois leadership that is, in its composition and its momentum, if not necessarily proletarian then plebeian; it's a popular movement. These bourgeois leaderships do everything possible to minimise the potential for social change, and limit the movement." [48]

Elsewhere, Boris Kagarlitsky wrote to the effect that "from the beginning, the ideological vector of the protests in the east has been different from that in the west. Left activists were driven from the Maidan in Kiev and beaten up...in Kharkov and Odessa, by contrast, Soviet monuments were defended, and here and there people even raised the red flag." He cautions that this is more an expression of cultural than class differentiation, but it leads in the direction of a democratisation of power in any event, with the central demand in the east being for an expansive measure of self-determination. [49]

Kagarlitsky has been criticised by some on the left for becoming an apologist for Putin, or at least for Russian nationalism. But his assessment of the forces on the ground that motivated the original uprising against Kiev in the regions of Donetsk and Lugansk is supported by other sources. Listen to the words of Sergei Chertkov, an official in the regional administration (Kiev-appointed) in part of the Donetsk region: "We are on the brink of an uprising of poor against rich, of chaos, of a terrifying rebellion". And he didn't mean that as a good thing – he is expressing a fear which unites all factions of the oligarchy in Ukraine. [50]

The top oligarch in Donetsk – Rikhat Akhmetov, who employs an almost incredible 300,000 workers in the region's mines and mills – certainly found he could not mobilise many of them when he tried to inspire a movement against the new authorities taking over in the Donbas. At his Enakievo Metallurgical Works, which employs 6,000, a pro-Kiev rally mustered only a few hundred despite management pressure, and ended after ten minutes. The head of the plant's trade union told a *Financial Times* reporter that "ninety-nine percent of the workers are against the Kiev authorities. Some want to be part of Russia, others want to be part of Ukraine, others want to be independent. But everyone is against the Kiev authorities, absolutely," he said. Their concerns, he added, were not just over the use of their language, but the new government's whole economic direction. [51]

Likewise, a spokesman for the left-wing Ukrainian party Borotba told an interviewer that "many miners and other working-class people" are fighting in the largest rebel units in Donbas. "These troops are fighting under red banners as opposed to others who use Russian, or even monarchist flags." [52]

Therein lies the core difference between those who rose up against Yanukovych in the west, and those who rose up against nationalism in the east. *London Review of Books* writer Keith Gessen went to Donetsk to report on the turmoil in summer 2014. He interviewed local lecturer, Yuri Degunov. "The protests in March and April were the most massive grassroots protests I have ever seen in Donetsk. In my memory people here had never been so active and so involved in their own fate."

Degunov "pointed out the very specific social composition of the protests in Donetsk. The pro-Maidan protests, when they took place, were middle class and nationalistic; anti-Maidan was lower class and anti-oligarchic (and Russian nationalist). The pro-Maidan protestors "expressed...barely concealed 'social racism' towards the members of anti-Maidan." [53]

That is towards people like Artur Smolin, who "has never lived in Russia. He was born in Ukraine in 1994...he grew up in the eastern Ukrainian town of Kramatorsk, roots for a Ukrainian soccer team and works in a Ukrainian factory producing machines for Ukrainian coal mines. But in early May, he took a bullet for Russia. Why? 'Because I'm Russian', he says." Or towards Artur Gasparayan, an Armenian from Spitak who travelled to fight alongside the Donbas rebels. "I don't consider Russia a foreign country. I have the mentality of a Soviet person. My grandfather fought for the Soviet Union and I am fighting for it," he said. [54]

Ukrainian political activist Peter Mikhailenko writes that "there are very concrete reasons why a large part of the population in these regions looks back to the Soviet Union as something positive...the people of Donbas have very real memories of their lives before and after the fall of the USSR. These memories include full employment, free quality education, free quality healthcare - all conquests of the working class." It may also reflect the fact that the tens of thousands of Donbas miners were privileged in Soviet times, earning high wages and retiring early. [55]

Volodymyr Ishchenko observes that "another particularity of the Donbas is that ethnic identity has historically been much weaker than regional and professional identities...They have always seen themselves as Donbas people or as miners first. In the western Ukraine it's the other way around: national identity is much more significant...The Maidan's tolerance for the far-right groups' veneration of Bandera was also a factor mobilising people in the east." [56]

Richard Sakwa also points out that the prevailing culture in the Donbas "appeals to neo-Soviet sentiments, recalling the good times of the Soviet period when jobs were plentiful, welfare (however minimal) was guaranteed and the borders between Russia and Ukraine were wide open, with numerous intermarriages and a genuine 'Soviet' people beginning to emerge." All this is, of course, anathema to the nationalists and neo-fascists of the western Ukraine. [57]

The attraction of the USSR, in the eyes of those who either lived in it or have had their lives shaped by its political-cultural inheritance, lies along two lines – the brotherhood of the peoples, and social security and stability, the two elements missing not only in the current crisis, but in the entire post-1991 history of the Ukraine (and most other former Soviet republics, including Russia, for that matter). The Soviet policy of inter-ethnic unity and solidarity may often have been honoured in the breach, and to have screened from view any amount of chauvinist backsliding with the Great Russian variety the most brazen, but its ideological impact should not be dismissed, and its present absence is a focus of considerable nostalgic longing, above all in areas like eastern Ukraine with a mixed national population. The impoverishment of the Ukraine, which has fallen far behind neighbouring Russia and Belarus since 1991, from a position of more-or-less economic parity, and the looting of its wealth by the rival oligarchies, scarcely need amplification as reasons for a further nostalgia for more secure and certain times which are still well within the memory of much of the population.

Alexei Mozgovoi – charismatic commander of a volunteer militia battalion in Donbas until his mysterious murder in May 2015 – exemplified these contradictions. Not a Communist, he nevertheless honoured the struggles and sacrifices of the Soviet people. He prioritised social justice for the poor and disadvantaged in Donbas, even as he fought against the Kiev regime's attack troops. But at the time of writing it seems to be as possible that he was killed by more right-wing rivals within the People's Republics – those more closely aligned with Putin and those who want to weaken Kiev without empowering working people – as by Ukrainian forces. [58]

This has obviously been no straightforward socialist revolution. Again in Kagarlitsky's words "the people who have been protesting against the authorities in Donetsk, Lugansk and many other Ukrainian cities have not had any particular knowledge of politics, or even a clear programme of action. The confusion in their slogans, along with their simultaneous use of religious and Soviet or revolutionary symbols, must undoubtedly offend strict connoisseurs of proletarian ideology" – including, doubtless, the wise leaders of the Fourth International and suchlike. All this has been concealed by the Kiev authorities, who would rather pretend that they face a Russian invasion than an uprising by their own people, with working-class people to the fore, which has largely confounded the efforts of the government to re-impose its own NATO-mandated "order" and usurped the state apparatus to a considerable measure. It also seems to have left Putin and Lavrov, who would not appreciate such a movement in Russia itself, somewhat uncomfortable, caught between their own class position and the patriotic petard they have erected and now risk being hoist upon. As Kagarlitsky says "this peaceful resistance will not only go down in history, but will also become an important part of the collective social experience of Ukrainian and Russian workers." [59]

The search for a third force – socialist, or at least genuinely democratic – which wants a Ukraine free from all forms of external domination, and also emancipated from the entirety of the oligarchic cliques which have exchanged office with each other since 1991 is understandably a sort of Holy Grail for some on the left. Such a search is often a vexing one in the post-1991 world, with the global retreat from socialism and class politics generally, and the resurgence of nationalist or religious-based ideologies. The working-class, defeated and atomised, is scarcely well-positioned either organisationally or politically to leap into the front rank with its own proposals for resolving the crisis in Ukraine.

This has undoubtedly weakened the uprising in the East, in the self-proclaimed People's Republics of Dontesk and Luhansk. The absence of a clear perspective beyond separation from the nationalists and neo-liberals in Kiev, and the bare facts of the intense military assault launched upon them have determined a dependence on Putin which has itself proved a weakness. The Russian government has not allowed the People's Republics to collapse, but it has ensured that any social transformation has been strictly limited, that they do not make any class-based appeals to other sections of Ukrainian working people, and that their development has been subordinated to Russian state policy, with its desire to be eventually welcomed back as a partner by the West as a factor.

As Kagarlitsky observed, the movement in Donbas "cannot survive without some cooperation with Moscow and the Russian government. And Russian elites use every opportunity to influence, manipulate and subvert these forces." Unavoidable support from the Russian government comes at a price, and one which is draining the "people's republics" of the Ukrainian east of their popular content. And according to the Borotba spokesman "the influence of Russia or, more accurately, the Putin administration is strong and even getting stronger....several military and political leaders, who came forward more or less spontaneously in the spring, have been removed and replaced by people who are more obedient towards Moscow." As a consequence, the movement in Donbas has drawn support both from elements of the European left, supportive of both the Republics' positive view of the Soviet experience and of their opposition to unbridled capitalism, and from part of the Putin-supporting far right, who admire his mix of nationalism and moral conservatism and who oppose the EU and all its works.

Nevertheless, two things can be ventured with some degree of confidence, and both should give pause to those in the western Left joining the EU and Washington in supporting the Kiev government today: First, if class politics do reappear as a decisive element in the Ukraine crisis, it will be from the peoples of the Donbas, and not from Lvov or Kiev; and second, a key element of their programme will be, by one means or another, the reduction or erasure of the boundaries dividing the workers in the Ukrainian state from those in the Russian. It is unclear on what socialist principle such cross-border solidarity could be denounced.

Whose?

If Russia had a plan to seize control of Ukraine, the overthrow of Yanukovych in February 2014 would have provided the perfect pretext. When the President fled Kiev, where he clearly believed himself to be menaced, to Kharkiv in the more hospitable east, he still remained the country's President, the blatantly unconstitutional action of the Rada in deposing him notwithstanding. Had he then asked for Russian military assistance, or been prevailed upon to do so, an invasion from the east would have had some genuine legal footing. Of course, masses of Ukrainians would have opposed such an act, but Novorossiya could doubtless have been brought under control – in Yanukovych's name – fairly swiftly. Yet Putin did little or nothing outside Crimea as the Ukrainian government tottered and fell unaided. It would seem that Russia did not have the designs on its neighbour which the West alleged. Indeed, the decisive action in Crimea aside, Putin's actions bear more the mark of vacillation, of being driven by events rather than mastering them, and of trying to navigate between aroused Russian national feeling on the one hand and the desire - intense among Russian business circles in particular – to remain a partner of the western powers.

It is of course clear that Russia could not remain an indifferent bystander to developments in Ukraine. Ties of business as well as history and geography connect the two states. In Richard Sakwa's words "Russia was not an external actor but an organic part of Ukraine's political economy." The two economies are deeply integrated – having indeed industrialised from the outset as part of one economic space, subject to the same Soviet planning directives. Heavy industry and the defence sector are particularly entwined, with common business interests straddling the new border between Ukraine and Russia. Pre-crisis, Russia accounted for around a third of Ukraine's trade. [60]

Many companies in eastern Ukraine, according to *The Financial Times* are "oriented eastwards, above all those working in its Soviet-era agricultural, metallurgy, pipe-making and defence industries." The President of Ukraine's Chamber of Commerce, Donetsk businessman Gennadiy Chyzhykov, pointed out that while the country exported raw materials and semi-finished goods to Europe, it send finished goods eastwards. "They share our tastes", he said. The interests of Gazprom, the Russian energy monopoly, in Ukraine need little elaboration – both as a strategic market and as an indispensable transit network, its desire for control over its neighbour's energy system is patently a factor driving Putin's policy. [61]

Had the European Union been driven by a real desire to see Ukraine's lot bettered, rather than by hegemonic aspirations, it would have seen Russia, with its substantial economic stake in a prosperous Ukraine, as a partner. Bush-era US National Security Council director Thomas Graham wrote that repairing Ukraine's state and economy "cannot be accomplished without Moscow's co-operation. Russia supplies the bulk of Ukraine's oil and gas. It accounts for a third of Ukraine's trade, and unlike Europe provides a market for its manufactured goods." [62]

Instead, discussions around Ukraine's association agreement with the EU became a zero-sum game. When Yanukovich suggested tripartite talks with both the EU and Russia, the Brussels bosses turned him down flat. EU Commission chief Jose-Manuel Barroso put it bluntly: "Russia's inclusion in the talks on setting up an Association Agreement between the EU and Ukraine is wholly unacceptable." Ukraine was thus obliged to make a choice and, since the deal offered by Russia was more attractive – given the country's energy dependence on its eastern neighbour, and the EU's insistence on eye-watering austerity as the price of association, it was always likely to be – it made a decision Barroso had not anticipated. Confrontation unfolded from that point, but it was not a confrontation that Moscow had appeared to seek. [63]

In fact, the claim by Russian Foreign Minister Sergei Lavrov that "Russia has done more than any other country to support the independent Ukrainian state" is not just self-serving diplomatic rhetoric. Russia has indeed subsidised Ukraine's energy requirements throughout the post-Soviet years, and its sensible proposal for three-way talks on the trade deal in November 2013 was flatly rejected by Brussels, doubtless with encouragement from the neo-cons still entrenched in the US State Department. Lavrov's view that building a new state in Ukraine required "the search for a balance of interests among its various regions, the peoples of which have different historical and cultural roots, speak different languages, and have different perspectives on their past and present, and their country's future place in the world," seems like no more than common sense, albeit one rejected or ignored by Ukrainian nationalists, the EU, Washington and conservative and liberal editorialists in London alike. [64]

It was all-or-nothing for Washington and the west, however. Since 1991, Ukraine had been a central target for western expansionism. Drawing it into the NATO/EU orbit was a guarantee against Russia recovering superpower status, profitable business in its own right as a country with major economic potential, and a pillar of US global authority as unchallenged superpower.

To that end, Ukraine has been the third largest recipient of US "aid" since 1991, after only Israel and Egypt. It was "the biggest prize" according to Carl Gershman, President of the US National Endowment for Democracy – not just a big fish to land in itself, but also a gateway to overthrowing the regime in Russia. The US invested over five billion dollars on democracy promotion in Ukraine since 1991, without achieving notable results apart, presumably, from establishing a broad client base among Ukrainian politicians. [65]

While Victor Yanukovych's first election as President of Ukraine – the one reversed in the "Orange Revolution" of 2004 – may indeed have been in part fraudulent, no-one seems to have disputed that his second election in 2010 was a fair reflection of the popular vote. His base was those millions of Ukrainians who identified with the Soviet past, or desired cooperation with Russia, or who otherwise rejected what became known as the "Maidan" version of Ukrainian identity. That, it seems, was simply not an acceptable democratic outcome for the USA, or the European Union. Democracy meant a system that would deliver

Ukraine to their hegemony, even if it meant utilising the nationalist far right to do so. Victoria Nuland, already encountered, was recorded dictating political outcomes for the Ukraine, including the composition of the post-Yanukovych government, at a time when the latter was still the country's internationally-recognised President.

It is unsurprising that Russia has resisted the unfolding of this scenario. It would take US power right up to its own borders and, as it turned out, mean the subordination of millions of Russian or Russian-speaking peoples to the ultra-nationalists driving the Maidan movement. It also had the potential to deprive the Russian Black Sea Fleet of its main, and historic, base at Sevastopol. It would be doubtful if any Russian government could survive such a series of humiliations on its own doorstep and, if there had been any doubt on the matter, Putin's response to the Georgian crisis in 2008 should have settled them.

That does not mean that Putin has no imperial ambitions of his own. He has made little secret of his desire to reverse some of the consequences of the Soviet break-up as and when opportunity presents, and his agenda is driven by the interests of the oligarchic class, particularly in the energy sector, and some of the state security elements he grew up with. He has sought to bring most of the former Soviet republics back into some form of special relationship with Russia on both security and economic questions by the usual range of big-power policies.

Former Polish Foreign Minister Radoslaw Sikorski – well-known in international neo-conservative circles – alleged that Putin had told Polish President Donald Tusk at a private meeting as long ago as 2008 that the two countries should partition Ukraine between them. Putin "went on to say that Ukraine is an artificial country and that Lviv is a Polish city... luckily Tusk didn't answer. He knew he was being recorded." One interesting aspect of this story, from which Sikorski subsequently tried to row back, is why he thought it was fortunate that Tusk knew his response would be on tape and therefore did not rise to Putin's bait. There is an implication that, had the alleged exchange not been recorded, Tusk (now President of the EU) might have not unequivocally spurned Putin's alleged offer, improbable as that sounds. In fact, the Polish population of Ukraine is today very small, largely as a result of the ethnic cleansing undertaken by the Banderaites during the Second World War and it is deeply integrated into Ukraine. Nevertheless, it is the case that if the Ukrainian state underwent a full-on disintegration (not likely but not at all impossible), Russia would not be the only external power staking a claim. One could also expect to hear from Hungary and Romania, and perhaps the Polish President will have found his tongue by then. [66]

Nevertheless, it seems most likely that the view expressed by *Guardian* columnist Seumas Milne that "Putin's absorption of Crimea and support for the rebellion in eastern Ukraine is clearly defensive and the red line now drawn: the east of Ukraine, at least, is not going to be swallowed up by NATO or the EU" is the right one. (67)

Putin's March 2014 Duma speech, already cited, mixes the militancy of an outraged Russian nationalism with a plea for understanding and a denial of any intent to set Russia up as a systemic opponent of NATO, whilst preserving its own strategic interests:

> "Today, it is imperative to end this hysteria, to refute the rhetoric of the cold war and to accept the obvious fact: Russia is an independent, active participant in international affairs; like other countries, it has its own national interests that need to be taken into account and respected.

"I also want to address the people of Ukraine. I sincerely want you to understand us: we do not want to harm you in any way, or to hurt your national feelings. We have always respected the territorial integrity of the Ukrainian state, incidentally, unlike those who sacrificed Ukraine's unity for their political ambitions. They flaunt slogans about Ukraine's greatness, but they are the ones who did everything to divide the nation. Today's civil standoff is entirely on their conscience....Do not believe those who want you to fear Russia, shouting that other regions will follow Crimea. We do not want to divide Ukraine; we do not need that. As for Crimea, it was and remains a Russian, Ukrainian, and Crimean-Tatar land. I repeat, just as it has been for centuries, it will be a home to all the peoples living there. What it will never be and do is follow in Bandera's footsteps!

"Crimea is our common historical legacy and a very important factor in regional stability. And this strategic territory should be part of a strong and stable sovereignty, which today can only be Russian. Otherwise, dear friends (I am addressing both Ukraine and Russia), you and we – the Russians and the Ukrainians – could lose Crimea completely, and that could happen in the near historical perspective...

"Let me note too that we have already heard declarations from Kiev about Ukraine soon joining NATO. What would this have meant for Crimea and Sevastopol in the future? It would have meant that NATO's navy would be right there in this city of Russia's military glory, and this would create not an illusory but a perfectly real threat to the whole of southern Russia. These are things that could have become reality were it not for the choice the Crimean people made, and I want to say thank you to them for this.

"But let me say too that we are not opposed to cooperation with NATO, for this is certainly not the case. For all the internal processes within the organisation, NATO remains a military alliance, and we are against having a military alliance making itself at home right in our backyard or in our historic territory. I simply cannot imagine that we would travel to Sevastopol to visit NATO sailors. Of course, most of them are wonderful guys, but it would be better to have them come and visit us, be our guests, rather than the other way round.

"Let me say quite frankly that it pains our hearts to see what is happening in Ukraine at the moment, see the people's suffering and their uncertainty about how to get through today and what awaits them tomorrow. Our concerns are understandable because we are not simply close neighbours but....we are one people. Kiev is the mother of Russian cities. Ancient Rus is our common source and we cannot live without each other.

"Let me say one other thing too. Millions of Russians and Russian-speaking people live in Ukraine and will continue to do so. Russia will always defend their interests using political, diplomatic and legal means. But it should be above all in Ukraine's own interest to ensure that these people's rights and interests are fully protected. This is the guarantee of Ukraine's state stability and territorial integrity.

"We want to be friends with Ukraine and we want Ukraine to be a strong, sovereign and self-sufficient country. Ukraine is one of our biggest partners after all. We have many joint projects and I believe in their success no matter what the current difficulties. Most importantly, we want peace and harmony to reign in Ukraine, and we are ready to work together with other countries to do everything possible to facilitate and support this. But as I said, only Ukraine's own people can put their own house in order." [68]

Here were the outlines of a compromise which provides the external context for resolving the crisis – full recognition of Ukrainian sovereignty, Ukraine as a state for all its citizens, cooperation between Russia and Ukraine, no annexations beyond Crimea, recognition of Russia's own interests, even cooperation with a NATO that does not seek to expand further - which at least some in the West are prepared to entertain. Thomas Graham, a former US diplomat once based at the Moscow Embassy, wrote: "The outlines of an accommodation are already visible: non-bloc status for Ukraine; decentralisation of the country's political institutions; some kind of official status for the Russian language; and an economic package drawing on US, European and Russian resources." Graham does not speak for official Washington alas. [69]

The idea of such an accommodation is anathema to a broad range of opinion – in Britain, above all. A militant anti-Putinism, which masks its lack of a single constructive idea for resolving the crisis with an excess of Cold War-style moral bombast, crosses the normal spectrum of differences. In the national press, it unites right-wing experts like Con Coughlin (*Daily Telegraph*) with bloviating centrists like Philip Stephens (*Financial Times*) and the liberal Natalie Nougayrede, who seems to have been engaged as a commentator by the *Guardian* for no purpose other than to whip European left-of-centre opinion into an anti-Russian front. For Stephens, it all seems to constitute a test of Europe's collective machismo. "The biggest danger to Europe comes not from the forays of Mr Putin's rusting aircraft carrier, or his cold war-vintage nuclear bombers, or from Soviet-style subversion in some of the darker corners of the continent. No, the real weakness lies in a European mindset that prefers to temporise and equivocate than to confront Mr Putin head on", he pontificates. What would head-on confrontation entail? And if Putin represents no real threat, why do it anyway? No answers from the oracle. It is the mindset of head-on confrontation, rather than the search for serviceable solutions, that threatens world peace. [70]

NOTES

1 http://www.washingtonpost.com/world/transcript-putin-says-russia-will-protect-the-rights-of-russians-abroad/2014/03/18/432a1e60-ae99-11e3-a49e-76adc9210f19_story.html
2 see Magosci p. 554
3 akwa, p. 153
4 Wilson p. 159
5 *Wall Street Journal*, 10 March 2014
6 Magocsi p. 377; Wilson p. 141
7 Maynar, pp 128-9
8 Wilson p. 16
9 Magocsi, p 574, 577, 579; see also Martin pp 75-124
10 Naimark p. 72, Stalin/Kaganovich p. 181; Martin pp 344ff, p. 356
11 Magocsi p. 609
12 *London Review of Books* 11 September 2014
13 Magocsi p. 714, 718; Sakwa p. 7
14 Wemheuer p. 212, 214
15 Wilson p. 145
16 Davies/Wheatcroft, p. 441; Wemheuer p. 216, citing Valin

17 Davies/Wheatcroft, p. 441; Naimark p. 77-79
18 http://www.infoukes.com/history/ww2/page-18.html
19 Gross p. 41
20 Gross p 29
21 Gross, p. 31
22 Jeremy Smith pp 134-5
23 Jeremy Smith p. 132
24 see Berkhoff pp 73-80
25 Berkhoff, p. 308
26 Grenkevich, p. 169, p. 230 and elsewhere
27 see Fyodorov
28 Berkhoff p. 312, citing Weiner
29 Wilson p. 161
30 *Guardian* 4 April 2015
31 *The Economist* 14 June 2014
32 Sakwa p. 62
33 *le Monde Diplomatique*, September 2014
34 Menon/Rumer p. 26
35 http://links.org.au/node/3752
36 *Wall Street Journal*, 2 March 2014
37 *Financial Times*, March 2 2014; *London Review of Books*, 20 March 2014
38 International New York Times, 24 February 2014
39 Sakwa p 123; *The Economist* October 25 2014
40 *The Economist* 23 May 2015; *Financial Times* 1 June 2015
41 *The Economist* 23 May 2015; *Financial Times* 16 April 2015; *Wall Street Journal* 11 June 2015
42 *Financial Times* May 18 2015, 11 August 2015
43 Wolfgang Munchau in *Financial Times* 27 April 2015
44 *Financial Times*, June 10 2015, August 1/2 2015
45 https://ukraineantifascistsolidarity.wordpress.com/page/2/
46 Newsweek 8 April 2015
47 *New Left Review* May/June 2014, p. 16
48 *Counterfire* interview by Feyzi Ismail, www.counterfire.org, 15 September 2014
49 http://links.org.au/node/3752
50 *Guardian*, 8 May 2014
51 *Financial Times* 20 May 2014
52 www.socialistaction.net, 9 January 2015
53 *London Review of Books* 11 September 2014
54 *Time* magazine, 19 May 2014; Sakwa pp 155-56
55 https://ukraineantifascistsolidarity.wordpress.com/2014/12/16/perspectives-for-the-peoples-republics-the-external-and-domestic-struggle-of-the-left-and-progressive-forces/
56 *New Left Review* May/June 2014 p. 25
57. Sakwa p. 24
58 see report by Eddie Dempsey, *Morning Star*, 27 May 2015
59. http://www.counterfire.org/index.php/articles/analysis/17203-boris-kagarlitsky-on-eastern-ukraine-the-logic-of-a-revolt
60 Sakwa pp 75, 13; *Financial Times* 10 June 2014

61 *Financial Times* 19/20 April 2014
62 *Financial Times* 28 April 2014
63. Sakwa p. 76
64 *Guardian* 8 April 2014
65 Sakwa p. 75
66 *Financial Times* 24 October 2014
67 *Guardian* May 1 2014
68 http://www.washingtonpost.com/world/transcript-putin-says-russia-will-protect-the-rights-of-russians-abroad/2014/03/18/432a1e60-ae99-11e3-a49e-76adc9210f19_story.html
69 *Financial Times* 28 April 2014
70 *Financial Times* April 10 2015

PART THREE
The Left and Ukraine

FEW WOULD deny that the Ukraine crisis is replete with the danger of a broader war – of the civil war in the Donbas, or the dispute over the Crimea opening up into a conflict which draws in external powers. At the very least, even if such a more general war is avoided now, and over this particular crisis, it seems more than likely that the forces and the circumstances which have got us thus far down the war road in Ukraine will get us still further down it somewhere else before too long, if left unchecked.

Those circumstances and forces, it has been argued here, grow out of the nature of contemporary imperialism, dominated and driven as it is by a US super-imperialism which seeks to expand its power, either directly or through multilateral bodies wholly or largely under its control, until it covers the whole globe. This drive to dominate, which meets the requirements of specific and quite easily identifiable class interests ruling the USA and its principal allies, interacts with local interests and contradictions in one place or another, which give each "flashpoint" its specific colouring. It also meets growing resistance, both from masses of people unwilling to be so dominated, or incorporated into Washington's sphere, but also from other state actors who, standing outside the super-imperial system, feel un- or under-represented in the prevailing global power system, and draw their own, movable, red lines against US expansion or entrenchment.

Ukraine represents the fifth major conflict in the space of fifteen years of this world order – Yugoslavia, Afghanistan, Iraq and Libya preceded it One could add Syria and Yemen too, although in both cases the intervention by the NATO powers has been masked or sub-contracted. These wars, and above all the Iraq invasion, have called forth an international anti-war movement in the heartlands and hometowns of imperialism of great strength, breadth and durability. At the heart of this movement has been what one can still call "the left" stretching from individuals and groups on the minority, left or pacific, side of social democracy through to trade unionists, Communists, Greens, far left and radical organisations and campaigners.

It is not axiomatic that that the left is always anti-war, or even opposed to the contemporary conflicts listed above. Particularly in Britain, where imperial traditions (liberal imperialist especially) reach deep into the labour movement and many sectors of the population, much of progressive opinion ends up, for a confection of rationalisations, supporting the state's interventionist role abroad. The NATO war against Yugoslavia, for example, was supported in Britain by the left-wing *Tribune* newspaper, at the centre of the Labour left for generations, and by the Scottish Trades Union Congress, traditionally a bastion of the left in the labour movement. Going a little further back, Britain's war with Argentina in 1982 received broad and intense backing on the left, on pretty specious "anti-fascist" grounds. Many far left groups evaded taking any position at the time, anxious to avoid getting on the wrong side of working-class patriotism.

Sometimes hesitation and confusion have been the result of contingent factors – the sudden emergence of a new movement, as in Libya in 2011, which it is difficult to immediately assess – but far more often the problems in securing effective and united progressive action lie in differing assessments of the nature of world politics, of the dynamics in the world situation, and the place of Britain within them. Historically, the left (in parliamentary terms) in Britain has been bedevilled by two problems in particular, which have persisted through several changes in the world – a progressive liberal interventionism, founded on the belief that Britain, alone or with allies has both the capacity and the duty to intervene abroad in good causes; and an Atlanticist outlook, which holds that Britain's place in international affairs is at the side of the USA, come more-or-less what may. Clearly, both of these outlooks have taken a severe knock this century, since liberal interventionism, over and above other objections which may be registered against it, has had the effect of making things far worse where it has been practised; and the policy of the Bush administration has had the effect of pushing even establishment politicians and strategists into reviewing the wisdom of unconditional allegiance to Washington. 1

The Iraq War represented a high-point of anti-war unity on the left. Still more importantly, it undermined support for "wars of choice" across broad sections of the British people. The establishment have been trying mightily to reverse this verdict ever since. The conversion of Wooton Basset, where bodies of soldiers who died in Afghanistan are returned to their home country, into a national symbol of support for the military formed part of this, as does the annual Armed Forces Day everyone is now enjoined to celebrate. And, of course, efforts have been made to wean the public back into war-fighting ways through finding conflicts susceptible to British intervention which people might still support. David Cameron famously came a cropper when parliament voted not to bomb Syria in 2013, an occasion which was surely at least in part rooted in a decade or more of powerful anti-war campaigning, and which has caused continuing apoplexy on the neo-conservative right.

This anti-war positioning is, however, fragile both in broad public opinion and on the activist left. The tug of establishment consensus and the hoary old view that where there is a problem in the world the British state has an obligation to "do something" both play a part. This has been reflected in responses to the Ukrainian crisis (as it has also been in relation to the Syrian conflict in some cases). Almost as debilitating are those arguments on the left which, while stopping short of calling for armed intervention by the British state, share and promote the political premises underpinning the government's attitude, or those which seek to take a half-way or equivocal view. All these arguments cripple the possibility of building a movement against the war danger – whether over Ukraine or the next conflict springing from the same sources down the road – and risk leaving public opinion at the mercy of the right.

The writings addressed here which express these views are only a selection. Many more could be found. In summary, they all represent different views on the world system today and different appreciations of imperialism and the structure of the world order it is struggling to maintain and extend, ranging from all-out support for the establishment approach through to a less brazen but perhaps more insidious anti-anti-imperialism, which takes as its point of departure the need to oppose any politics which prioritises resistance to Empire, and those who do challenge imperialism but make no priority of challenging the Anglo-American variety of it.

Left-Foot "Lies"

Left Food Forward is one of the better-known blog sites in and around the Labour Party, and James Bloodworth is its editor. He is a consistent neo-imperialist of the left, combining support for a social-democratic agenda at home with resolute backing for the Transatlantic world policy of the Bush-Blair era. He gets to write in the *Wall Street Journal* from time to time too, a high accolade in such circles. Bloodworth was deeply disappointed by the failure of the war against Syria to get moving in 2013, and even more disappointed at the role the Labour Party played in preventing it, but not so disappointed as to actually leave the Party over the issue, unlike Blairite *Telegraph* pundit Dan Hodges. He represents the continuation in the purest form of those few on the media left who supported the invasion of Iraq in 2003 (Christopher Hitchens, David Aaronovitch, Nick Cohen etc)

Unsurprisingly, he has been a strong critic of Russian policy in relation to the Ukrainian crisis and has demanded a robust response by Britain, the EU and NATO. Towards the end of March 2014 he posted a piece on his website entitled "5 persistent falsehoods about events in Ukraine". It is a revealing article. [2]

Bloodworth's "Lie Number one" (all these purported lies, it should be said, emanate from the "Russian propaganda machine", which he identifies as being constituted of the TV station *Russia Today* and *Guardian* columnist Seumas Milne) was that the EU/NATO 'provoked' Putin. A minor quibble here is that Bloodworth attacked "the Russian annexation of Ukraine", an event no-one else had spotted.

More importantly, he excused EU and NATO policy of any part in generating tensions with Russia, not just in relation to the Ukraine, but over the entire post-Cold War era. He argued that the expansion of NATO, in particular, has corresponded to the wishes of the people of the countries concerned. Up to a point, this may be true. Surely the Baltic states and Poland, for example, do not wish to see a return of Russian-directed government (although even here a nostalgia for the real benefits of the socialist system persists). However, there are several problems with this benign narrative (the guarantees NATO gave Moscow in 1991 that it would not so expand among them), the most salient for our purposes is that neither the government of Ukraine nor very many of its people wanted what was on offer.

Bloodworth did not address the deeply divided nature of Ukrainian public opinion on the EU issue. It does not matter as much that Russia does not want Ukraine to draw closer to Brussels but that a very large number of Ukrainian people themselves see it as abhorrent. Common sense would indicate that a better relationship with both the EU and with Russia would at least help the country hold together. But it was the EU which turned the trade talks into a zero-sum choice. The draft Treaty prepared by the EU would have precluded Ukraine also joining the Eurasian Union, a customs bloc promoted by Russia, by far Ukraine's largest economic partner. Furthermore, the EU Commission head Manuel Barroso and President Herman van Rompuy refused a proposal by Yanukovych that the talks turn into a three-way negotiation, including Moscow alongside Kiev and Brussels. This was neither respecting Ukraine's sovereignty nor a prudent course of action, unless the whole purpose was to extend the EU and NATO's influence (the Treaty also had a security component) not only at the expense of Russia but also in the teeth of the view of Kiev's own elected government and either a majority or at least a large minority of the people of the country.

The next "lie" a la Bloodworth is that the Ukrainian government is fascist. On the face of it, Bloodworth is right – the government in Kiev as of spring 2014 was broadly nationalist, representative of a range of Ukrainian-nationalist opinion but not of that 40% of the country, at least, which does not identify with the "national project". Its biggest element was drawn from the party of former Premier Yulia Tymoshenko, corrupt and Russophobic but not itself fascist, and the biggest influence on it was its western patrons, for whom fascist groups are a tool to be discarded when its purposes have been served. It does, however, include some overt fascists, some of whom could qualify as national-socialist in ideological inspiration. Bloodworth and others on the left treated this far too lightly, as the subsequent apparently unstoppable rise of the undoubtedly fascist Right Sector has shown.

Indeed, Bloodworth's rebuttal of this "lie" was curious, in that he apparently conflated fascism with anti-Semitism, and then announced that the presence of Jews in the new government means that it cannot be fascist. All along the line, this is a parade of ideological non-sequiturs. He cites a rebuttal of allegations of "anti-semitism" in the new government by one Jewish leader in Kiev, but does not as much as allude to contrary observations made by other Rabbis in the City. In fact, the existence of a powerful strain of anti-Semitism in Ukrainian nationalism, and in the western Ukraine from where the new government draws most of its support in particular, is a fact undisputed by anyone with even a passing knowledge of the country and its history.

These forces were at the time most vocally represented in the new government by the Svoboda Party (formerly the Social National Party of Ukraine), described on Channel Four News as "a fascist party styled on Hitler's Nazis" as well as the street-fighting Right Sector. The World Jewish Congress has called on the EU to ban Svoboda. Svoboda regards itself as the followers of wartime Ukrainian nationalist Stepan Bandera, whose organisation, the OUN-B, committed the anti-Semitic atrocities already detailed during World War Two. One OUN-B leader Yaroslav Stetsko declared that "I...support the destruction of the Jews and the expedience of bringing German methods of exterminating Jewry to Ukraine." And the OUN-B suited word to deed, killing an estimated 30,000 Jews, alongside many thousands of Poles and pro-Soviet Ukrainians too.

As for the Right Sector it is, *inter alia* and perhaps unsurprisingly, firmly "against same-sex marriage. The Gospels are the most important part for us," in the words of a spokesman quoted in the *London Review of Books*. That is worthy of particular mention in order to highlight that those who led the justifiable criticism of Russian law on the same subject in the run-up to the Sochi Winter Olympics, and who normally miss no chance to challenge religious fundamentalism in politics when the religion in question is Islam, are silent on this point too in relation to the NATO-backed Ukrainian authorities. 3

And were those parties actually in power when Bloodworth wrote? The Secretary of the National Security & Defence Council, Andriy Parubiy, hailed from Svoboda, as did deputy Prime Minister Oleksandr Syoh and the new ministers for Ecology and Agriculture. Even more disturbingly, Parubiy's deputy at the Security Council was then Dimitri Yarosh, the leader of the Right Sector. Add in that the new Prosecutor-General Oleh Makhnitsky, was also a Svoboda member, and we can see that already in March 2014 the far-right was establishing strong positions in the security and legal apparatus, a process which is far from having been reversed since.

Nor were clear indications of neo-fascist behaviour lacking. The post-Yanukovych parliament had already passed bills banning the Ukrainian Communist Party (its offices in Kiev had been destroyed and the home of its leader set on fire), repealing the ban on Nazi propaganda, placing Right Sector activists on the staff of the Interior Ministry and repealing the official use of minority languages, including Russian. It is true that some of these agreed proposals were not put into effect thanks to western pressure, and also true that there were counter-efforts (far from successful ones), also driven by the western powers, to at least end the domination of the streets by illegal armed groups. If Svoboda has lost support since, it is in part because of the overt displays of the Nazi-type behaviour which Bloodworth appeared unaware of.

The sight of US Republican senator John McCain shaking hands with fascists in Kiev requires little explanation – all questions of political propriety are subordinate to the interests of forming an anti-Russian front in Europe, in the interests of US power, for such as him. The question here is why does Bloodworth and the like choose to see no fascists when they are governing in plain sight? Why, for example, does disgraced ex-MP Denis McShane (also active in spreading pro-Kiev and anti-Russian publicity), who has campaigned against the rise anti-Semitism in Europe in recent times, ignore the alarming presence of anti-Semites in a European government in his comments on the Ukrainian crisis? The conclusion must be that in part their virtuous campaigning is contingent, and can be over-ridden by other strategic considerations for imperialism, which is a point worth remembering the next time they ascend their high horses.

Third of the Bloodworth-identified "lies" was that Former Ukrainian President Viktor Yanukovych was overthrown in an 'illegal coup'. Bloodworth's description of the deposed President as a "corrupt autocrat" stimulates little dissent, although when he cast doubt on the integrity of Yakunovych's election in 2010 he broke new ground, since in fact that poll (unlike the one in 2004) was universally regarded as broadly fair. By these means Bloodworth tried to evade the fact of the overthrow of a democratically-elected leader by means of violent street protests.

Did Yanukovych deserve to be sent packing? No doubt – he was both corrupt ('even by Russian standards' in Putin's faintly bizarre characterisation) and unfastidious in his political methods. But that neither makes the means of his overturning constitutional (nor prudent, given the scale of support his party has in much of the country); nor does it confer on the successor regime any legitimacy. As Marina Lewycka wrote in the *Guardian* "Yanukovych, for all his grotesque self-enrichment, was democratically-elected, as few of the self-appointed government have been." 4

We have already considered the replacement regime, which Bloodworth enthusiastically supported and which has offered nothing at all as a sop to his social-democratic illusions.

Of course, the nature of the post-Yanukovych power installed in Kiev does not make Yanukovych himself any better than he was. But the new regime had no more legitimacy than the old – essentially one group of presiding oligarchs was replaced by another, with no more public support than the ousted leader. Those people in the Maidan movement genuinely demanding a liberal democracy have already lost. But this did not seem to bother Bloodworth at all.

Russians living in Crimea are in danger – this was the fourth "lie". On this, Bloodworth is clearly right. The threat to Russians living in the Crimea (and elsewhere in Ukraine for that matter) stopped well short of that, although given the undoubted presence of fascists and other Russophobes in the Kiev cabinet and coercive apparatus, the fear that it could get worse is not entirely fanciful.

Protecting Russians in Crimea was, it is fair to say, not one of Putin's priorities, as opposed to one of his excuses. Preservation of the base of the Russian Black Sea fleet in Sevastopol would undoubtedly have been the main concern of Russia's rulers. Furthermore, the annexation presumably relieves Russia of the obligation of paying the eye-watering rent (between 40 and 45 billion dollars apparently) negotiated for the lease on the base by Yanukovych, whose alleged orientation to Moscow did not extend as far as passing up a good opportunity for loot.

However, addressing this lie without addressing the underlying truth – that most people living in Crimea now and for twenty-three years past would rather be citizens of Russia than Ukraine – is pointless. Had the Russian annexation of Crimea been resisted to any extent at all by anyone, no doubt the matter would have a different complexion. But that did not happen, and it is an omission that cannot solely or even mainly be attributed to intimidation. The result of the referendum may have been exaggerated, but 95% of an 80% turnout supporting union with Russia, or about 77% of the population on the peninsula, is a long way from implausible. In fact the views of the Crimean people who, like many others across the former Soviet Union "woke up one morning in the wrong country", did not seem to figure in Bloodworth's analysis at all. Like fascists in Kiev, they disappeared as an inconvenience to the neo-con narrative.

It was with the fifth and final "lie" that Bloodworth got to the heart of the matter. This was that there is a moral equivalence between the actions of the West and those of Russia/Crimea which demonstrates the West's 'hypocrisy'. Indeed, the mere suggestion of any equivalence between Russia's actions and the West's breaches of national sovereignty seriatim reduces all neo-conservatives to spluttering indignation.

In a way, Bloodworth was right – there is no equivalence. For Putin's annexation of the Crimea to bear comparison to NATO's Kosovan aggression would have required Russia to have not merely marched troops into the peninsula causing a grand total of one death, it would have demanded the sustained bombing of Kiev, the destruction of the Ukrainian energy and industrial infrastructure, thousands of civilian deaths and the dropping of munitions on the Chinese Embassy in Kiev to boot.

Since appealing to international legality can't spring him from this particular trap, Bloodworth distinguishes between legality and "legitimacy", the latter being amenable to entirely subjective definition in his handling. The Kosovan operation was made legitimate by Serb depredations against the Albanian population there, while absent such beastliness in the Crimea, Russia's move is not "legitimate". The actual views of the people in either case are immaterial to Bloodworth, as is the point that, for Crimeans, the transfer of their land from Russia to the Ukraine in 1954 had no legitimacy.

There is little to be gained in disputing the point with someone who so readily moved off the relatively secure ground of the law regulating international conflict into the marsh of each state's concept of what it considers "legitimate". The principle of might-is-right is already conceded here, and anyone who imagines that this right can, will or ought in future to be exercised by NATO powers alone, as was the case between 1989 and 2008, is living in a fool's paradise. If a US invasion of Iraq is "legitimate" then a Chinese invasion of Taiwan would be still more "legitimate" since, unlike Iraq, Taiwan is not an internationally-recognised state. And so on. No-one will regard Putin's conduct in Crimea as a bigger crime than the Bush-Blair invasion of Iraq, and rightly so.

Bloodworth regards all this as "whataboutery", as in arguing "what about so-and-so" rather than dealing with the matter in hand directly. "Whataboutery" actually strikes to the heart of the debate about the creation of any just and sustainable world order. That is, the rules of any such order must apply to all. Bloodworth has the right to believe that the system and way of life in the USA and Britain is the best presently attainable, and that its governments can be trusted with a scope of action and powers which should be denied other less favoured countries. But if he expects the rest of the world to share that view and accept that Washington, London and Paris must uniquely have the right to intervene where they will on the assumption that their causes alone are automatically "legitimate", then he is profoundly blinkered. Either – international law observed by all; or a free-for-all in what is now a multipolar world. The days when the Bloodworths bestrode the world unchallenged, clothed solely in their own sense of "legitimacy" and moral superiority, are finished forever.

And in his final sentence, which itemised "what Tony Blair had for lunch" after Kosovo/Iraq in a list of what he regards as irrelevances, he only revealed the supercilious callousness of the callow neo-con, who could equate wars in which hundreds of thousands have died with a Prime Minister's dining habits as issues to be equally ignored. That is one reason, at least, why so much of the world rejoices in any development which constitutes a setback, however ill-intentioned, to the hubris and hypocrisy of Anglo-American power.

My enemy's enemy...is mine too

The view that the real problem in Ukraine is Russia, that Muscovite imperialism is the main aggressor, and that the left should therefore back the "Maidan movement" and the Kiev regime, albeit with some respectable reservations, has gained some currency. Two expressions of it have been presented by Tim Nelson of the International Socialist Network (ISN) and Liam MacUaid of Socialist Resistance. The ISN was a recent breakaway from the Socialist Workers Party (it has now apparently dissolved itself), while Socialist Resistance is the British affiliate of the Fourth International.

Nelson argues that "the anti-imperialist consensus has largely broken down" on the British left. This is the one indisputably correct assertion in his article. He goes further and states that "the Stop the War Coalition has become politically bankrupt", but laments "we are not in a position to build a new campaign", which may be as well. The breakdown of consensus finds fair reflection in his article, which takes as its main target the slogan – correct in 1914, but outdated today – "the main enemy is at home". Nelson argues that "the First World War was an all-out conflict between rival imperialist camps. While Western imperialism has no doubt been encouraging Ukrainian nationalists in the hope of facilitating a turn towards the European Union sand away from Moscow, the main aggressor, both historically and currently, is Russia." Ukraine has been oppressed by both Russia and the USSR and "the Maidan movement is simply the latest attempt to break Ukraine from Russian domination."

Following this logic, Nelson simply ignores the role of the EU, NATO and Washington in the present crisis. They are unseen, non-players. The whole matter reduces to Ukraine and Russia. And in this, opposing the Kiev government must not be the priority because "there is an important distinction between right-wing nationalist and conservative capitalist governments, and a fascist one", and the Kiev regime is the former. Svoboda, "has a number of rabidly anti-Semitic leaders and racist policies" and is perhaps "far-right populist", but it is not fascist, and not a "dictatorial party which aims to found the state on racial grounds."

This is a casserole of confusion. The distinction between far-right populism and fascism is a specious one historically, nor does fascism require the establishment of a "racial state" to declare itself as fascism. The logic of Nelson's argument is that everyone in the Ukraine should suspend anti-fascism until and unless the Kiev regime finally declares itself as fascist – by which time it might well be thought to be too late (echoing the passivity of the German social democrats in 1932 as the Bruning dismantled democracy prior to Hitler's takeover). In the meantime, despite a "right-wing nationalist and conservative capitalist government" sitting in power, the main concern should be – Russia, and "Russian separatists."

As things are, this non-fascist government has banned the Communist Party in much of the country and excluded it from parliament, it has unleashed massacres in Odessa and Mariupol, is deploying such of its coercive forces as can be mobilised against working people in the east, is institutionalising the honouring of wartime Nazi ally Stepan Bandera and is host to not just "right-wing populists" in its ranks but also to those, like Right Sector, who even passes muster as fascist on planet Nelson, although, he assures us "its relationship with the government is at best complex."

The truth is that for Nelson, as for Brussels and Washington and the open neo-conservative Bloodworth, the extreme nationalist and proto-fascist nature of the Kiev regime is, like the interference of the EU and the US in Ukraine, and their sponsorship of the new government, an embarrassing element to be obscured in the interests of the fight against the main enemy. Nelson is not ambiguous here – "the first step for the self-determination of all Ukrainian people has to be the immediate withdrawal of Russian troops and an end to its interventions in the country's politics". Not a word about ending the Ukrainian government's war on sections of its own people, nor about ending the gross and sustained interference by the world's greater imperial powers. It is perhaps superfluous to mention that the role of the British government, of Cameron and Hague, does not get a single mention in his review.

It is this logic which leads Nelson, uniting the Ukrainian crisis with the Syrian civil war, to conclude that "the Stop the War Coalition argument that 'the real enemy is at home' ceased to be a principled anti-imperialist position, and became nothing more than apologism [sic] for Putin's Russia and the regime [in Syria] he supports. This is not internationalism, as the real enemy for the people of Syria was not the US, but al-Assad and the Russian state backing him. The same is true for the Ukrainian people now." Alas for him, neither the Syrian nor the Ukrainian people have sub-contracted to the erstwhile International Socialist Network the job of determining for them who their "real enemy" is. It seems plain that if all the Syrian people took Nelson's view then the Assad regime, for all its depredations, would not be still standing. And plainer still that the more than 40% of the Ukrainians who voted at the last asking for parties advocating closer links with Russia do not see their "real enemy" to the east either. [5] If Nelson covers the European Union in a veil of discretion, no such inhibitions bother his Socialist Resistance co-thinker Liam MacUaid. The latter positively celebrates the European Union. Here is his panegyric to the EU and bourgeois democracy: "For many Ukrainians all that is good about the outside world is represented by the European Union. From their point of view, and that is what matters here, joining the EU means that they might have a chance to get a job in England, Germany or Belgium. In a country in which virtually every transaction between a citizen and the state means paying a bribe, the EU can seem like a corruption-free paradise. Singing a song which mocks the government doesn't get you thrown in jail….Contrast that with Putin's treatment of Pussy Riot. Who wouldn't choose to live in a society like Denmark when the option on offer is living in a client of Putin's Russia."

Let us not dwell on the fact that MacUaid's EU, unlike the real one, has apparently not spent the last five years imposing austerity in Spain, Ireland and Portugal and subverting democracy in Italy and Greece, nor that the Brussels bureaucracy is a by-word for corruption (its accounts have not been signed off by the auditors for years), nor even the more dialectical point that most of what are transactions between "citizen and state" in Ukraine (and indeed lubricated by graft) are styled market transactions between consumer and corporation further west, and none the more exalted for that. We can even pass over the fact that the Rolling Stones were (briefly) jailed in 1967, and would no doubt have been imprisoned for longer had they ascended the altar, Pussy Riot-style, at Canterbury Cathedral during Easter service to sing "(I Can't Get No) Satisfaction." Nothing is going to shake MacUaid's devotion to western liberalism in its various manifestations.

No, the larger objection is that Ukrainians "from their point of view" do not hold the views he attributes to them. Millions clearly do feel an affinity with Russia (with a per capita GDP three-and-a-half times that of Ukraine, this need not be a matter of tradition alone), or at any event feel none with the Kiev government installed by the sanitised EU of MacUaid's imagination. MacUaid has an answer to this objection to, lest it place in doubt his role as self-appointed spokesman for the Ukrainian people. It is a variation on the same position advanced by every benign colonialist when confronted by evidence of the ingratitude of the subject population. In his own words - Ukrainians' consciousness "has been evolving rapidly from a primordial swamp of old prejudices, half-remembered ideas and glimpses of the outside world." Poor swamp-dwelling Ukrainians – how different they are from the enlightened erudition and panoramic sweep of the savants of the Fourth International. All MacUaid's chauvinist snobbery asserts is that he, in fact, would rather live in liberal bourgeois Denmark than primordial prejudice-infested proletarian Donetsk, and this is a choice he should not be prevented from exercising whenever he wishes. 6

Like Nelson, MacUaid explicitly sees the most desirable outcome in Ukraine as being a defeat for Russian imperialism. He assures us that "if the EU or NATO were to start making claims on Russian territory we would oppose that." In the same fashion as Nelson would oppose fascism in Ukraine once it was undeniably established, but not before, MacUaid would challenge NATO once it becomes openly colonialist, but no earlier. Since NATO and the EU have never made an overt territorial claim on anyone, and since imperialism stopped using such claims as it main form of expansion some seventy or more years ago, there need be no concern in Washington or Brussels that they will have to face any opposition from Socialist Resistance on this matter any time soon. Happily for them, the attitude of both factions towards anti-fascism and anti-imperialism appears to take its inspiration from St Augustine (O Lord make me chaste, but not just yet...). And since the EU and NATO have cunningly operated in the Ukraine and elsewhere on the basis of formal respect for existing state boundaries, their role and interests are not worthy of further examination, so MacUaid does not bother with one.

One should note parenthetically here that the same Fourth International factions – Socialist Resistance, the ISN and others – have also jointly called for the supply of arms to the anti-Assad forces in the Syrian civil war. Of course, in a world where the EU is a beacon of democracy, where there is no fascist threat in Kiev and where the USA is a bit-part player in the Ukraine it is just possible that the authors of this position believe that this does not amount to a call for imperialism to arm the opposition, thereby ineluctably take full control of it, to prolong the conflict and then install their own clients in power in Damascus. In the parallel universe dwelt in by the rest of us, it seems clear that the ISN and Socialist Resistance have abandoned the actual fight against western imperialism and are moving instead in the opposite direction.

Enemies Everywhere, and Who's to Choose?

The position of the SWP, an organisation at the very heart of the mass anti-war movement from 2003-7, is somewhat different. If the Fourth International offer objective backing to the Kiev government and its international sponsors, the SWP offers support to no-one and nothing. The article by Alex Callinicos outlining this position is considerably more erudite and insightful than those considered above, although inevitably marked by his tradition's (mis)reading of Soviet history. Nevertheless, he lays due weight on the emergence of inter-imperialist rivalries, and rightly scores the record of the Ukrainian elite since independence. "Politics in Ukraine is the continuation of gangsterism by other means" he observes. On the Maidan movement, Callinicos's characterisation of its elements is free from the dewy-eyed fantasies of the Fourth International, acknowledging its "illusions in 'Europe'" and its "important opening to the extreme right". He describes the coup that brought down Yanukovych as "the latest twist in Ukraine's corrupt game of Tweedledum and Tweedledee." [7]

However, when he comes to orienting the left or the anti-war movement, Callinicos swerves to avoid the difficult issues, not a swerve as sharp as the Left Unity factions, who are more-or-less overtly backing western imperialism and its allies, but sharp enough to avoid making Washington and London the main focus of opposition. He takes his stand on Trotsky's unfortunate call in 1939 for the Ukraine to be separated from the USSR (in the same article in which the latter also proclaimed the impossibility of Ukraine ever uniting under the auspices of the 'Stalinist bureaucracy' a few short months before this unification actually happened, confirming that the exiled prophet was losing his prophetic mojo by that stage). From here, Callinicos decrees that Crimea's claim to separate from Ukraine (with which it was not united in Trotsky's time in any case) is "extremely dubious", demands that "Putin's apologists on the western left" denounce his conduct over Chechnya (which many of course did at the time) and then warns that any Russian move into eastern Ukraine would be met by a "nationalist insurgency there". To confound Callinicos, no more prophetic than Trotsky it seems, what has actually happened is that Kiev regime troops have moved into eastern Ukraine to confront a popular and *anti-nationalist* insurgency instead. It would seem that the working people of Donbas are just about the only insurrectionists in the last fifty years not to have met with the SWP's approval.

But the core of Callinicos's argument is that the left focuses too much on opposing US imperialism and neglects to oppose all imperialisms. The US is in relative decline, there is now a more fluid period of competition between great powers opening up, and contestation of US hegemony is rising, he writes. All of that is true up to a point, but it is an important point. The US remains overwhelmingly the major block on social progress and self-determination worldwide. It is the only global imperial power, enjoying a hegemonic position even now, when the "unipolar moment" has passed, far greater than Britain held before 1914. It accounts for as much military spending as the next ten states put together. It is the only state with the capacity to intervene anywhere in the world – indeed the Pentagon has a separate command for every continent and ocean on the planet. It directs to all intents and purposes all the main institutions of ultra-imperialism (NATO, IMF, World Bank, WTO etc). In the course of this century alone, US imperial power has sent a vast army around the world to invade Iraq, has occupied Afghanistan, has launched drone strikes in violation of the sovereignty of numerous states with impunity, has sponsored or supported regime change in other countries, and has begun to gird itself for confrontation with China.

By contrast, Russia is barely able to reassert itself as a regional power. If it is an imperialist state, it is a most primitive one. It is far from being able to reassemble the elements of the old Soviet Union, much of which had been run by Russia under the Tsars for decades or even centuries. The idea of it projecting its power back into the heart of Europe is quite implausible. It struggles to hold on to slivers of territory outside its existing borders. Its famed Black Sea Fleet is puny compared to the US sixth fleet in the Mediterranean. That does not mean that Putin's actions are unimportant, or that local issues generated by the very partial reassertion of Russian power can be discounted – but it does mean that on the world scale the US remains the overwhelmingly dominant imperial power, the main enemy of progress across the globe (something well recognised by most states and peoples and grudgingly acknowledged by Callinicos). Just as importantly, in the context of a movement working within the main ally and partner of the US in most of its crimes and adventures, the focus of anti-war campaigning should be turned on its actions, including in the Ukraine today. The enemy of the British anti-war movement is indeed "at home" – a government entwined with the Washington world imperialism, not with the Muscovite regional power.

It is this last point which is the main weakness of the SWP's analysis. It stands outside the actual alignments in the world, judges all powers by the same standard and denounces them all equally, as if in Britain our tasks vis-à-vis Putin are the same as they are vis-à-vis Cameron and Hague. Given the actual place in the world of British imperialism and its relationship to the USA, that constitutes an abdication.

The same position, more-or-less, is taken by RS21, another group which broke away from the SWP in 2013. Analysis of international politics do not seem to have been the point of rupture. In a polemic against the Stop the War Coalition, it argues that the main enemy is whoever is obstructing a particular revolution at a particular time, irrespective of more global considerations. In this setting, they find US aggression diminishing:

> "The neocons are not in charge of the White House and the obsession with them is mistaken. The aggressive imperialism they stood for was always a gamble based on exploiting a temporary window of opportunity. That's what the Project for a New American Century was all about. That window has passed. Applying a 2004 analysis of the US ruling class to 2014 simply won't wash.
>
> "Today, Obama's administration has its sights set on the challenge of China. Its "pivot" to Asia has seen the development of alliances in the region and temporary deployments of troops as the US seeks to concentrate 60% of its military power in the region.
>
> This does not mean that the US has abandoned its interests elsewhere. One has only to consider its attitude to the Arab Spring, particularly its involvement in the bombing of Libya, to see that. However, military involvement by the US has not been the main enemy of revolutionaries in the region. For Syrian revolutionaries, the unstinting support of Russia and China has allowed Assad's regime to frustrate the revolution, drawing it into armed conflict and slaughtering tens of thousands." 8

More explicitly than Callinicos, this excuses the activities of the US in the Middle East (where it still deploys enormous military force) and relegates its "aggressive imperialism" to the past. It also alleges that Putin's support for Assad has been worse for Syria than the continuing backing offered to a variety of "moderate" and jihadi opposition fighters, not to mention the bombing of the country by the USA. Let's just say that none of these propositions are self-evident – to see Russia rather than the USA as the main problem facing those seeking progress in the Middle East is an attitude which could only be held by either apologists for western imperialists or those employing ultra-left rhetoric (seeing revolutionary movements where they no longer exist) to avoid making tough choices. They do all have the effect, in Ukraine and the Middle East, of giving Washington a free pass and downplaying its role as the main instigator of conflict and backbone of counter-revolution anywhere in the world.

My enemy's enemy is my friend

The slogan "the main enemy is at home" is criticised from the opposite direction to Nelson/MacUaid by Paul Roberts of Socialist Action – an organisation which has played an important part in the anti-war movement and all recent struggles against imperialism more generally. Socialist Action's outlook is miles away from the liberal imperialism now affecting some far-left groups. All these strengths are fully reflected in Roberts' article, which correctly directs its fire at western imperialism's eastward expansion.

Roberts is keen to acquit Russia of being an imperialist power. This is an argument which has a touch of scholasticism, since Roberts acknowledges, as does everyone, that Russia is a capitalist country, and further allows, in relation to the Chechen question at least, that the Putin government can follow a reactionary policy. Now if we have a large and powerful capitalist country pursuing a reactionary policy against other peoples in its own neighbourhood or elsewhere, then one could be tempted to simply say that imperialism is as imperialism does.

The arguments Roberts musters to establish the non-imperialist nature of Russia are scarcely conclusive. It has a much lower per capita GDP than the USA or Britain – that was true in 1914 as well, when Lenin denounced the Tsar's imperialism. After 1991 "a large part of Russian manufacturing industry was smashed by competition from the west", which is true but only decisive if a huge manufacturing base (and Russia's is still substantial) is regarded as a sine quo non for being imperialist. This is scarcely true today, and if it is Britain too would be cleared of the charge, our own industry substantially reduced and our own imperialism dependent, as ever, on the role of the City of London rather than the conquest of manufacturing markets. "Russia has not sought foreign colonies or to dominate semi-colonies abroad", Roberts says, a statement which over-simplifies greatly imperialist methods of domination today and would again excuse contemporary France or Britain, let alone Germany or Japan, from being imperialist states. In fact, Russian policy towards Kazakhstan and Kyrgyzia, for example, does indeed have a neo-colonial colouring. Gazprom has recently acquired the Kyrgyz gas network, Rosneft (another Russian energy giant) has taken control of the country's main airport and Russian state-owned electricity firms are building power plants there. There is also a Russian military base. Indeed, Russia has more bases outside its own territory (Syria, Tajikistan among them) than Japan does, for example. Kazakhstan too is kept closely in the Russian orbit. These arguments against the possibility of an emerging Russian imperialism are flimsy, and at most only establish the obvious – that Russia is a primitive and relatively weak power. [9]

A more substantial case is argued by Roberts: "Imperialism is a structured international economic and political system guaranteed by the US at its core. Its imperialist partners, like Britain and France, share responsibility for the imposition of imperialist rule through military force....There is no parallel imperialist organisation from Russia. It is excluded from the club of imperialist countries imposing and maintaining the world order, to which it is subject." This argument is correct in that identifies the US-led world system as the main and most important expression of imperialism today. However, it denies the possibility of any imperialism arising outside of that system, and hence any salience in the 21st century of Lenin's position on inter-imperialist rivalry.

There is a purely empirical critique of this position, in that Russia under Putin has been very anxious to be included in the US-dominated "club of imperialist countries". As Boris Kagarlitsky has noted, the "people in power in Moscow are as liberal and pro-western as they can be given the current mood in Russia. Their only goal is to be friends of the West, and to send their children and their money to London and Zurich." 10

Indeed, unlike China, Russia lobbied successfully for the G7 to become the G8, until its recent punitive exclusion. It provided full support, including logistical, for the US invasion of Afghanistan in 2001 and afterwards, and it gave the green light to NATO's attack on Libya (although it subsequently regretted this). So until the Ukraine crisis erupted, Russia was half in the club, and well-placed for full membership.

But Roberts' formulation is also open to more profound objections – imperialism is not a structured system, however much it might like to be, unless you are going the whole hog with the theory of ultra-imperialism and believe, like Hardt and Negri, that it is already a consummated fact. It is a competitive and dynamic system which changes and reorders over time, often but not exclusively through war. Even if Roberts' description of the present imperialist system and Russia's relationship to it was accurate, a further reordering inspired by new "shut out" powers is sooner or later inevitable, just as the pre-1914 Pax Britannica system, structured as far as could be, unravelled under the pressure of rival empires. The fact that Russia has not erected its own "parallel imperialist organisation" to those established by Washington and its allies does not mean that, having failed to break into the US-led system sufficiently, it will not instead work unilaterally and with others to break out of it. One can certainly make a case that such a break-up is a good thing on balance, regardless of the motivations of those doing the breaking, but it should not mean closing one's eyes to the class and social essence of the regimes challenging the world order. Roberts' position could only make sense if Russia and the Russian ruling class are regarded as semi-oppressed, and incorporated in the US world order in a position analogous to that of Argentina or Egypt. That seems to considerably understate Russia's actual strength and position, as well as the clear signs that it does indeed wish to create its own "sphere of influence" where the power of other imperialists is excluded or severely limited at the least.

Moreover, if it is accepted that Russia is capitalist, then certain things follow. Capitalism was re-established in Russia on the basis of a very high degree of monopolisation, inverting the long-held argument that capitalist monopolisation made the transition to socialist planned production easier at the economic level. Oligarchic rule was immediately based on very large companies in the energy and defence manufacturing sectors above all. These firms were closely tied in to the new private banking sector, since it was via the banks that the crooked privatisation of Soviet state assets was implemented in Russia. These newly-privatised firms of course inherited very close links with similarly-privatised companies in other former Soviet republics, Ukraine included – the re-establishment of those connections has been a priority for Russian economic policy, serving as it does the interests of the new ruling oligarchy. This is, in my view, the sketch of an emerging, if backward, imperialist power.

Of course, that is debatable. However, when the conclusion is drawn by Roberts that the left in Russia should be supporting the policy of Putin in Ukraine we move into even more contentious territory. There is no basis for admiration for the Putin regime. Unlike the old USSR it does not represent a different social system. It is unquestionably capitalist, of a particularly corrupt and oligarchic sort. Putin's ideology is a mixture of Russian nationalism and Orthodox-inflected social conservatism. It has very limited international appeal, and such following as it has includes big elements of the European far right. Putin's success has been to stabilise first the Russian ruling elite, and then the wider society, after the devastation of the Yeltsin years. He has consolidated capitalism by trimming its most lurid oligarchic excesses and curbing democratic rights alike and has gradually reasserted Russia's sphere of influence, mainly by exploiting legitimate grievances of citizens left stranded by the partition of the USSR in 1991. To place trust in such a government – which is no firm friend of the movement in Donbas and has in fact acted to curb the latter's radical potential, and which speculates on rather than expresses the real democratic demands of Russians and Russian-speakers outside Russia's borders – is to separate mechanically support for national demands from their social content. It is to assume that the opposition to imperialist expansion from the west can be entrusted to the oligarchic elite, with one eye on their Knightsbridge mansions and their London bank accounts. In Russia, as elsewhere, the "enemy is at home", and it is the ruling oligarchy and its reactionary ideological positions.

Nevertheless, this position does not have the negative consequences for political campaigning which the other attitudes described here do. It allows for a focus on US and British imperialism as the main problems to be confronted. It is far distant from the politics of the far left factions still stuck in the cold war "neither Washington nor Moscow" groove. As Mao Zedong might have said, it is a contradiction amongst the people. But the left must retain the capacity to recognise imperialism when it emerges, and to see beyond the present alignments of world power to identify the dangers of the future too.

The difficulty with Roberts' position is therefore a tactical one, not one of principle. Uniting against the super-imperial power is surely correct – that is the only way that countries and people across the world will really be able to exercise national and social self-determination. However, to align anti-war campaigning with authoritarian rulers, proto-imperialist or not, will only make such work harder.

The challenge posed by the other positions discussed is a more fundamental one. They all avoid taking a stand against the super-imperial world system centred on the USA and Britain as the main focus of anti-war campaigning. This opportunism makes no sense, in that it is from there that the wars of this century have sprung, and future ones are most likely to. That is true of Ukraine to, if one looks beyond the headlines. It is the relentless expansion of that world system, in spite of the setbacks it has encountered, which has put Ukraine "in play".

The basic attitude of the anti-war movement should be conditioned by one position above all – opposition to the US-led imperialist bloc of which Britain is a major part, operating through NATO and the EU. This bloc constitutes the main roadblock to general human progress in all continents today. It is the "world order" which has invaded Iraq, Afghanistan and Libya, which seeks to dominate all states regardless of the wishes of their inhabitants.

Without its power being diminished or broken, any form of democratic or social advance is sure to be limited, blocked or reversed. Least of all in Britain should we occlude this fact, since peoples across the world depend in part on our campaigning here to help create better conditions for their own emancipation.

NOTES

1. see Murray, 2009
2. http://www.leftfootforward.org/2014/03/5-persistent-falsehoods-about-events-in-ukraine/
3. *London Review of Books*, March 20 2014
4. *Guardian*, March 10 2014
5. http://internationalsocialistnetwork.org/index.php/ideas-and-arguments/international/war-and-imperialism
6. http://socialistresistance.org/6085/ukraine-the-russians-are-the-aggressors#comment-66203
7. http://www.isj.org.uk/index.php4?id=959&issue=142
8. http://rs21.org.uk/2014/03/24/ukraine-four-points-in-response-to-chris-nineham/
9. *Financial Times*, June 10 2014; *Guardian* May 5 2015
10. www.nytimes.com, September 8 2014

CONCLUSION

Stare into the abyss and the abyss stares into you - Nietzsche

THE UKRAINE crisis has pushed the world closer to the abyss of war. As of August 2015, fighting was continuing in the Donbas between rebel forces and Ukrainian government troops. The Western powers persisted in blaming Russian aggression for the whole conflict, ignoring both the indigenous divisions in Ukraine, the provocative actions of the Kiev government and the consequences of NATO and EU expansion alike. Sanctions put in place against Russia since the takeover of Crimea remain in force and are doubtless impacting on the Russian economy. A long-term solution to the Donbas rebellion and the broader divisions in Ukraine seems elusive.

This malaise is typical of the deterioration of the "new world order" which the USA has sought, by persuasion or ultimately imposition, to create since the end of the Cold War. Far from new, this order is in fact now fast reproducing the pathologies of the European past. Great power conflict is back on the agenda in Eastern Europe and the Far East, and re-emerging in the Middle East, too, amidst the wreckage of the occupation of Iraq and the thwarting of the "Arab Spring".

More than ever, this demands a united and powerful response from the anti-war movement across the world, Britain included. A programme to resolve the Ukrainian crisis is not hard to itemise:

The first demand should be to stop the eastward expansion of NATO and US military power, including a halt to the deployment of US or British armed forces to Poland, the Baltic Republics or elsewhere in Eastern Europe. Such deployments are no more than sabre-rattling, and preparations for a new war in Europe.

The second demand should be for an end to any British government support for the war the Kiev regime is waging against its own people in Donetsk, Lugansk, Odessa, Mariupol, Slavyansk and elsewhere. This is a war without a shred of democratic legitimacy which risks sparking a civil war at the least, and perhaps a wider conflict.

Thirdly, there should be a democratic solution to the Ukrainian crisis, with the different regions being offered the opportunity to decide without any coercion whether they are happy with the constitutional status quo, or would prefer federal autonomy, independence or, where such a thing would be possible, union with Russia. Let the voice of the people be heard, and let there be respect for the choices freely made. Any view that the post-USSR frontiers should be set in stone are ahistorical and, since they can only ultimately be maintained against the popular will by force, a recipe for war.

This should be combined, in Britain, by a consistent exposure of the role of the British elite; its support for the extension of a European Union that is helping impoverish millions across the continent, its work hand-in-glove with Washington in the push to extend NATO neo-colonialism while preserving the City of London as banker and bolt-hole of choice for the corrupt oligarchic capitalists on all sides. The elite's support for policies leading to war must be confronted.

This dovetails with the need for a broader programme that addresses the imperialist system from which the crisis has sprung. Ultimately, this is a global cause. Whichever form of imperialist system is proving decisive, its roots are the same – monopoly capitalism and its impulsion to utilise the state apparatus of the G7 powers, including the military, to sustain and reproduce the conditions for securing greater profits in a crisis-ridden world economy.

It is not possible to revert to a pre-monopoly capitalist economy. Despite all the Chicago School posturing, the days of the pure free market are history. But the depredations of the decisive sectors of capitalism, which constitute the heart of the imperialist system, can be addressed even short of the establishment of socialism. The energy sector, the financial system and the arms industry can be taken into public control and be made publicly accountable for their conduct. While nationalisation is no guarantee on its own of good behaviour – then state-run BP's role in helping engineer the overthrow of the progressive Mossadeq government in Iran in 1952 is evidence of that – it can certainly create greater possibilities for oversight and a democratic tempering of their engagement with government and foreign policy in particular. Such public ownership, particularly of energy suppliers and of banks, would have other economic benefits for the British people too.

Any advance for democracy is also antipathetic to imperialism. Greater parliamentary control over the government's war-making powers helps, as the House of Commons decision not to bomb Syria in 2013 showed. Pressure for observance of international law and acceptance of the authority of the United Nations are further steps in the direction of curbing, although not stopping, moves towards war.

Underlying any of this must be the understanding that, just as the illusions of a post-1991 world order of global peace have been shown demonstrably false, so too the idea that wars will always be fought "somewhere else" and that the British people will suffer but little from acts of war undertaken by the government around the world will prove unfounded.

Ukraine should bring these points to the forefront of politics. It is the distillation of every factor making for a general war and as such the call-to-arms for a programme and a movement to prevent it.

Bibliography

Ali, Tariq	*The Extreme Centre* (London: 2015)
Arrighi, Giovanni	*Adam Smith in Beijing* (London/New York: 2007)
Beria, Sergo	*Beria, My Father* (London: 2001)
Beria, Lavrenti	*On the History of Bolshevik Organisation in Transcaucasia* London: 1935)
Berkhoff, Karel C.	*Harvest of Despair* (Cambridge, Mass./London: 2004)
Bukharin, N.I.	*Imperialism and World Economy* (London: 1972/1917)
Boron, Atilio	*Empire & Imperialism* (London/New York: 2005)
Boterbloem, Kees	*The Life and Times of Andrei Zhdanov* (Montreal: 2004)
Coggan, Philip	*Paper Promises* (London: 2011)
Davies, R.W, Oleg Khlevniuk and E.A. Rees (eds)	*The Stalin-Kaganovich Correspondence 1931-36* (New Haven/London: 2003)
Davies, R.W. and Stephen Wheatcroft	*The Years of Hunger* (Basingstoke: 2009)
Day, Richard B.	*The 'Crisis' and the 'Crash'* (London: 1981)
Donald, Moira	*Marxism and Revolution* (New Haven/London: 1993)
Faux, Jeffrey	*The Global Class War* (Hoboken: 2006)
Fine, Ben and Alfredo Saad-Filho	*Marx's Capital* (London/New York: 2004)
Foster, John Bellamy and Robert McChesney	*The Endless Crisis* (New York: 2012)
Fyodorov, Alexei	*The Underground Committee Carries On* (Moscow: 1952)
Gamble, Andrew	*The Spectre at the Feast* (Basingstoke: 2009)
Grenkevich, Leonid	*The Soviet Partisan Movement 1941-44* (London/Portland: 1999)
Gross, Jan T.	*Revolution from Abroad* (Princeton: 2002)
Hale, John	*The Civilisation of Europe in the Renaissance* (London: 2005)
Hardt, Michael and Antonio Negri	*Empire* (Cambridge, Mass./London: 2000)
Hilferding, Rudolf	*Finance Capital* (London: 1981/1910)
Hobson, J.A.	*Imperialism* (London:1988/1902)
Jack, Andrew	*Inside Putin's Russia* (London: 2004)
Kiernan, Victor	*America: The New Imperialism* (London/New York: 2005/1972)
Krugman,Paul	*End This Depression Now* (New York/London: 2012)
Lapavitsas, Costas	*Profiting without Producing* (London/New York: 2013)
Lendman, Stephen (ed.)	*Flashpoint in Ukraine* (Atlanta: 2014)
Lenin, V.I.	*Imperialism, the Highest Stage of Capitalism* (Moscow: 1952/1917)
Ligachev, Yegor	*Inside Gorbachev's Kremlin* (New York: 1993)
Luxemburg, Rosa	*The Accumulation of Capital* (London/New York: 2003/1913)
Magocsi, Paul Robert	*A History Of Ukraine* (Toronto: 2010)

Mandel, Ernest	*Late Capitalism* (London/New York: 1978/1972)
Martin, Terry	*The Affirmative Action Empire* (Ithaca/London: 2001)
Marx, Karl	*Capital*, volume two (Harmondsworth: 1978/1885)
Marx, Karl	*Dispatches for the New York Tribune* (London: 2007)
Marx, Karl	*The Poverty of Philosophy* (Moscow: 1975/1847)
Maynard, John	*Russia in Flux* (London: 1941)
Menon, Rajan & Eugene Rumer	*Conflict in Ukraine* (Cambridge, Mass/London: 2015)
Milne, Seumas	*The Revenge of History* (London/New York: 2012)
Murray, Andrew	*Flashpoint: World War III* (London/Chicago: 1997)
Murray, Andrew	*The Imperial Controversy* (London: 2009)
Naimark, Norman M.	*Stalin's Genocides* (Princeton: 2010)
Porteous, Tom	*Britain in Africa* (London/New York: 2008)
Rachman, Gideon	*Zero-Sum World* (London: 2010)
Reich, Robert	*Supercapitalism* (London: 2009/2007)
Sakwa, Richard	*Frontline Ukraine* (London/New York: 2015)
Screpanti, Ernesto	*Global Imperialism and the Great Crisis* (New York: 2014)
Smith, Jeremy	*Red Nations* (Cambridge: 2013)
Smith, David	*The Age of Instability* (London: 2010)
Stalin, J.V.	*Marxism and the National Question* (Moscow: 1936)
Tett, Gillian	*Fool's Gold* (London: 2009)
Wemheuer, Felix	*Famine Politics in Maoist China + the Soviet Union* (New Haven/London: 2014)
Wilson, Andrew	*The Ukrainians* (New Haven/London: 2009)
Wood, Ellen Meiksins	*Empire of Capital* (London/New York: 2003)

www.ingramcontent.com/pod-product-compliance
Lightning Source LLC
Chambersburg PA
CBHW072048160426
43197CB00014B/2680